MW01234385

How to Travel for Free (or pretty damn near it!)

Global nomads tell you how to do it

Updated 2nd Edition

By Shelley R. Seale and Keith Hajovsky

Table of Contents

"The world is a book and those who do not travel read only one page." ~St. Augustine

FOREWORD

This book is the second edition of *How To Travel For Free (or pretty damn near it!)*. It is the updated and revised version of our original book, which was published in 2010.

With this revised edition, we have updated the book to give more examples of some of the free (or close to it) travel that we have done in the last three years. We have also updated all of our resources, links and tips – and added many more resources and methods that are new to the market, or that we have discovered and utilized ourselves.

We hope you enjoy this updated edition, and get more inspiration and practical tools than ever to make your travel dreams a reality! You can also keep up with us, and a constant update of new resources and opportunities for free or cheap travel, at:

- Our blog: http://howtotravelforfree.net
- Facebook: http://facebook.com/HowToTravelForFree
- Twitter: http://www.twitter.com/travelfreebook

"One's destination is never a place, but a new way of seeing things." – Henry Miller

INTRODUCTION

Hi, I'm Shelley – a freelance writer, author, and self-professed vagabond. My curiosity about the world and love of travel started early and runs deep, and I will rarely miss an opportunity to discover a new place, culture, people and way of life.

My partner, Keith, has traveled throughout much of the United States and nearly 50 different countries on 5 continents. As his friends and family

Keith & Shelley in Nicaragua, just before volcano boarding. January 2012

will tell you, he loves to travel, and always focuses on getting the most out of his travel dollars so that he can explore just that much more.

There are many travel resources and guidebooks out there that tell you how to travel on the cheap, how to save money, how to get the best airfares. We have read and used many of them, and there are lots of good ones around. This one is different in that in these pages, we share our own personal resources and experiences to show ways in which you can travel not just cheaply, but for free – or damn close to it.

While we won't claim to have traveled the entire world – the more we travel the longer our list of destinations grows – between the two of us we have traveled extensively throughout our little planet over the past two decades, and over that time we have both discovered that you don't have to spend a lot of money to travel. In fact, we often travel to exotic places for very, very close to free. The more we've traveled, the less we've spent.

For example:

♦ In 2004 Keith said goodbye to his job and headed out for Asia. He wasn't sure how long he would be gone – he figured until he got tired of traveling or ran out of money. By the time he came back home to Austin, it was 2006 and he had been gone for two years

– on surprisingly little money, and without any trouble in picking up a new job just where he'd left off. In fact, he found potential employers to be impressed and envious of his two-year sabbatical.

♦ In November 2008 I took my mother to Hawaii, where we spent two weeks for about the same money it would have cost us to stay home. We used frequent flyer miles for the airplane tickets and stayed in a private two-bedroom condominium found through a home exchange. In July 2011 I did the same thing in Montreal, taking not only my mother but also my daughter and nephew – all on frequent flyer miles and staying in a home exchange. I spent a week on my own in San Miguel de Allende, Mexico, at a casita home exchange and a United miles ticket. I recently returned from another practically-free family vacation: 10 days in San Diego, California with my mom and daughter, using miles tickets and staying in a beautiful four-bedroom house, on an exchange.

♦ In April 2009 Keith and I spent several weeks in a studio apartment in Barcelona, steps from the famed Ramblas – completely free, courtesy of another home exchange. We did the same thing in March 2010 in a two-bedroom apartment on the Upper West Side of Manhattan; a downtown Seattle condo in June 2011; and a week-and-a-half in Granada, Nicaragua in January 2012. We have used this method for free vacations in Paris, Venice, Mexico, Vancouver, Portland, Los Angeles and right here in our home state of Texas.

People ask both of us, *all* the time, how do we do it? They are admiring, envious, impressed, and mystified. They sigh and say, "I wish *I* could travel for weeks or months, like you do." But the truth is, most of the people who say this have *far* more financial means than either of us do. This brings us to the first lesson of this book, a rule to remember:

Money is, by far, *not* the primary requisite for world travel.

Creativeness, time, planning, resourcefulness, and a totally different mindset are all far more valuable attributes in traveling for free, or as close to it as possible.

So how do we do it, personally? We are going to tell you exactly, in this book. And we should also let you know, before we even get started, that neither of us are independently wealthy, or famous; we do not have a network of rich and famous friends or any other store of resources that the average person does not have. Far from it, in fact – we are both self-employed freelance workers with relatively modest incomes. Although we have chosen to create work and lives that prioritize mobility and travel, we still have many "normal" facets to our lives and do not possess any secret resources that anyone can't utilize.

I have a daughter, and am a homeowner and pet owner. Although I have been mostly self-employed for many years, Keith had a regular 9-to-5 job up until five years ago, and has been self-employed since then. And still, we have both managed to travel extensively, often for no more than what we would spend by staying at home, or very little more. And if you travel a few months or more at a time you can actually do so while spending *less* than what you would spend had you stayed home.

For Keith and I, a few basic life choices have been instrumental to our current lifestyle:

1. **We don't believe in job "security," and in fact feel that climbing the corporate ladder can lead to golden handcuffs that prevent one from leading the life they really want to lead.**

2. **We purposely crafted work around the type of life we want to have: namely, location independent and friendly to our desire to travel frequently.**

3. **Our home-based lives and homes in Texas are low maintenance and cost; we feel that the more "stuff" you own, the more it begins to own you. While we do have homes and stuff, we try to keep it pretty minimal and maintain a low overhead, with few bills and avoiding the trap of building up debt.**

4. **We prioritize our choices of where we want to spend our money. For us, travel is the biggest priority. Rather than spending our disposable income on expensive clothes, salon visits, brand new cars, fancy restaurants or cable TV, we prioritize the bulk of it on travel. After all, happiness comes from relationships and experiences – not from things.**

None of this happened overnight. This was the result of years of building our work, getting rid of stuff and bills, and slowly working toward a more minimalist home base and location independent work. Because that's the life we wanted to have.

But you may not want that. You may not want to travel as frequently or as long as we do; you may not have a desire or a need to create an entirely new lifestyle or change your job to accommodate long-term travel.

This book is for anyone who simply wants to travel more, for far less money. Whether you want to set your life up to go for weeks or months, or even years, at a time – or whether you simply want to find out how you can take close-to-free vacations a few times a year – we are here to show you how we do that.

We should also take a minute to define what constitutes free travel, for us. **It doesn't mean that you will globetrot without ever spending one single penny.** We will be the first to admit that's pretty much impossible, and we want to address our definition of "traveling for free" because over the past few years of this book and our blog, we have gotten a lot of comments and questions about this from people saying essentially, "What are you talking about? There's no way to travel *entirely* for free!"

Yes, we agree.

Standing on the Equator in Ecuador, July 2013

There's pretty much no way to *live* entirely for free, either. **To us, traveling for free means that we are able to travel for less money than we would spend if we didn't travel at all. To see the world on a lower budget than we would spend if we simply stayed at home.** If we are in Asia or Africa or South America (or wherever in the world) for weeks or months at a time spending less money than we would have spent had we not gone on the trip at all — that is free travel to us. And we make it happen, on a continual basis. We make it happen through a variety mix of methods and resources. Sometimes we have rented our own place out back home, earning money to finance the trip — or we've simply exchanged homes, staying somewhere else for the same cost as staying home. Usually we've scored free plane tickets through airline points, or bartered out work for travel. We often travel in places that cost far less than the U.S., giving us a lot more for our dollar. Usually it's a combination of many of these methods — all of which we share with you, in detail, in this book!

We also want to share, in fact stress, this aspect of free (or close to it) travel that we have experienced:

Traveling for far less money does not mean a lesser experience.

**In fact, it can create a richer experience that
connects you far more with the place.**

While some people may feel that extreme budgeting will limit their travel experience, we have found that people can not only still have a good time on a much tighter budget, but can actually have more meaningful and enjoyable trips by planning their travel in different, more creative ways.

For example, Keith cites a trip we took a couple of years ago to New York City. If money was less of a concern perhaps it would have been easier for us to just make reservations at a hotel and eat out at whichever restaurants we might hear or read about. Instead, I set up a home exchange with someone who has an apartment in the Upper West Side, and we ate at the apartment for most of our meals while still eating at some really great restaurants at discounted prices via Restaurant.com and daily specials that we had read about. We also found great performances and live art or music shows that were free or heavily discounted.

And you know what? It ended up being the best time either of us ever had in New York! The apartment we stayed in had lots of old New York personality and charm. Likewise, we really enjoyed shopping at the little local markets for food to cook for our meals. And most of the restaurants we did indulge ourselves with were really terrific. We did the whole three-week trip on an extremely tight budget considering it was New York City, and didn't feel like we missed out on anything. We actually felt like we had a more genuine Big Apple experience than if we had stayed in a swanky hotel downtown.

So the moral to story is that you really *don't* have to spend huge amounts of your precious income to have a great vacation. It is a myth worth forgetting that you have to spend a lot of money to travel well. Many of our favorite travel memories have been cultural interactions that came about because we stayed in a local home or neighborhood, traveled by public transportation, and indulged in inexpensive local activities. Because in the end what we are all looking for in a trip is personal satisfaction, and if we can achieve that by traveling more intelligently and with more thought then all the better not only for our bank accounts but also for our own happiness and fulfillment.

This book is our own personal account; exactly how we do it, along with additional resources we have picked up from fellow travelers, friends, travel writers, and the hundreds of travel books, magazines and websites we've read or written for. It is not meant to be a comprehensive guidebook of everything cheap-travel-related, but more of a handbook of our own personal resources and tips.

We have also laid out the book in a way that will, hopefully, allow it to become a resource workbook for you, as well. There are places for notes, travel planning, checklists and other additions that you may want to make; the purpose of this book is to make it your own, utilize it, and use it well when planning your own fantastic, adventurous, amazing and *free* or nearly-free journeys!

Travel well!

"Our battered suitcases were piled on the sidewalk again; we had longer ways to go. But no matter, the road is life." ~Jack Kerouac

HOW TO USE THIS BOOK

While the book is broken down into chapters about the different major aspects of travel – transportation, accommodations and creative ways to travel – in each section you will find the following useful tools sprinkled throughout. You will also see some references followed by a number – these correspond with the Website Reference List at the end of the book.

Websites
When you see this icon, you will find a list of what we consider the most helpful websites on the topic being discussed on that page, for further information and to help with your planning.

Tips & Advice
This icon represents a place where we insert a personal experience that one or both of us had with the subject matter, resulting in a "lesson learned" that we will pass on to you.

Testimonial
Don't take our word for it! When you see this thumbs-up icon, another traveler besides Shelley and Keith shares their story of how they use a method or resource to travel for free.

Planning
Here you will find a half-page or page that is dedicated to planning tools for your use, such as checklists, research and itinerary confirmations.

Brainstorming
These are the most fun spaces! At the end of each section is a space where you can jot down some of your best travel ideas, spurred by prompts that will get you thinking about where you want to go and what you want to do.

"The true voyage of discovery consists not in seeking new landscapes, but in having new eyes." ~Marcel Proust

BEFORE YOU GO: SHELLEY AND KEITH'S CHEAP TRAVEL BASICS

In order to get the most out of the concept of traveling for free or pretty damn near it, we want to share three basic axioms that we live by, *before* you even start planning your next trip. Keeping these things in mind can greatly affect how, when and where you plan to travel, and just how cheaply you can do so.

YOUR MONEY OR YOUR TIME

There is a saying in the business world that a product or service can be good, fast, or cheap. A customer can choose two out of three of these things to have, but she can't have all three. We have found that there is a similar axiom to travel, which brings us to our next rule:

You will sacrifice either time or money, and you have to decide which.

There are those who have enough money, and are willing to spend whatever it takes, to have a great vacation; presumably you are not in that category since you are reading this book! There are also those who will spend more than is necessary on packaged vacation and retail rates, because they don't really have the time to research, investigate and plan. Then there are people who spend more than they have to, simply because they don't know how to go about traveling for free or next-to-nothing. We are here to unlock that door and let you into the club, but you have to be aware up front that what you are giving up in exchange for free or cheap travel is the time you will have to invest to do so.

If you have the extra time and don't mind spending it, both on research and planning and while you are traveling – you will travel for the least amount of money. The less time you have or are willing to spend, the more money you will part with. There is a direct correlation between the two.

Time spent in researching ways to travel for free, contacting people, and planning your journey will, of course, translate into the most travel for the least amount of money; however, this relationship between time and money exists just as much *while* you are traveling.

LONG-TERM AND SLOW TRAVEL = CHEAPER TRAVEL

Many people marvel at how long we often travel for – a month, two months, or longer. And this is nothing compared to Keith, who once spent almost two years vagabonding around South Asia! Obviously, for both of us this is in large part due to our work situations – Shelley is a self-employed freelancer and Keith took his Asia journey while between jobs. We concede that not everyone with regular jobs and set vacation time can do this (see the *Jobs, Vacation Time & Sabbaticals* section). However, with employers, vacation time and ability set aside, there is a major rule of travel that many people don't seem to grasp:

The longer you travel, the less expensive it becomes.

Sounds contradictory, right? But it's true. We can travel for two months in Central America or much of Asia for less money than most people would spend on a one week vacation – and have, many times. Keith traveled for a month in Laos for less than $500, and had an amazing time. International airfare is one of the biggest travel expenses; once you've arrived somewhere faraway, getting around in that country or continent

via buses, trains and low-cost airlines is usually remarkably inexpensive. When you do enough research to combine modes of travel in a way that takes advantage of the cheapest choices – and when you can be flexible enough with which dates you go where – the cost of transportation per day plummets dramatically.

We call this *slow travel*. That $900 airfare to Greece can be parlayed into added excursions into Eastern Europe and Southern Asia with little additional expense. And the second largest travel expense, lodging, also takes a nosedive the longer you stay. Renting a flat, vacation condo or even hostel is significantly less expensive when you're renting by the week or the month. Of course, the goal is to not pay for housing at all whenever possible, and we'll look at many sure-fire ways to do that.

Besides the cost savings, there are several other huge advantages to traveling for longer periods of time rather than shorter vacations. For one thing, it's much easier on the environment. Carbon emissions from airplanes, as well as vehicles and trains, are one of the biggest negative impacts of travel. The more we can plan to avoid multiple flights and combine them into longer journeys, the better it is for the planet and all of us humans living on it. Which brings us to the second part of that rule:

The slower you travel, the more meaningful and less expensive it becomes.

Slow travel reaps so many additional benefits for you, the traveler. When you take more time, when you stay longer, when you travel slow, you see more. You get to experience things you wouldn't have otherwise, and that most people never get to. You're able to explore, to take your time, to truly get to know a place and its people – and you are able to relax more, because you aren't spending half your time racing from place to place. You attain a deeper level of understanding and immersion into the local culture and flavor. You meet more locals and get to know and appreciate them better. You would be surprised at how often a favorite memory comes from some tiny corner of a place, some interaction with a local, and not from a hurried tour around a major attraction site.

If you love to travel as much as we do, and if you've already traveled much, you probably already know exactly what we're talking about. Tourists leave home to escape their world, while true travelers leave home to find it. When you only have a very short time to "vacation," by necessity you will spend the majority of time in the most touristy areas of a place. There are two major drawbacks to this: First, these are always the most expensive places to be, and in some countries, visitors can spend more money in one week

flickr.com/photos/sharpshutter/

than many locals will make in a year. Second, these tourist zones most often consist of a sort of "show" that is put on to attract visitors, rather than an authentic experience of what the people, place, history and culture are really all about. *These two drawbacks define the proverbial "tourist trap."*

The opportunities for authentic travel increase a thousand-fold when you travel slower, and longer. When you are in a place long enough to explore its nooks and crannies, and share true experiences with the locals, you come to know what is valuable to them, and understand the place in a way that is denied conventional tourist vacationers. It allows us to have the sort of experience we long for, the reason we really leave home for in the first place, and this can be life-transforming. We highly encourage you to try and do this as much as possible. Even if you have a traditional job and scheduled time off, there are ways to do this more through combining vacations and days off, sabbaticals, and other creative travel ideas that we will explore in that section on page 83.

WHERE YOU GO MATTERS

Just like spending more time researching and planning your travels, taking longer trips, and traveling more slowly, deciding *where* you travel can also make a big difference to the average daily costs of your trip. The costs of accommodations, meals and other expenses vary greatly throughout the world – Central America and much of Southeast Asia are generally *far* less expensive places in which to travel than Europe, North America and much of South America.

PriceOfTravel.com is a fantastic resource for finding out the costs of traveling to different countries all over the world. Their annual Backpacker Index is extremely helpful, whether you are a backpacker or a luxury traveler or anything in between. Tim Leffel's Cheapest Destinations Blog (1) is another great resource for finding out which countries are best for stretching your precious travel dollars.

For example, Shelley took a work trip to Switzerland in 2013 and had a fabulous time in that beautiful country. Luckily for her though that trip was all-expenses-paid, since it was for a journalism assignment. Because, as expected, she noticed that the prices for just about everything in Switzerland were really high. She said that a burger and soda lunch at a casual restaurant ran $25, and the price for just one beer at the most sought-after bar in lavish St. Moritz was $40!

At the other end of the spectrum, we traveled together in Panama for a couple of weeks only a few months before Shelley's trip to Switzerland. On that trip we likewise had a fantastic time and saw quite a bit of yet another beautiful country. However, we averaged only about $6 each for lunch meals at mid-range restaurants, bought fresh ceviche at the fish market in Panama City for $3, and on the coast in Bocas del Toro found a great little bar called Toro Loco where ice-cold beers only cost $1! We could have easily spent months in Panama for what just one or two weeks would cost in Switzerland.

The point of that comparison is to show you just how widely your average daily expenses can vary depending on which exact country or countries you are traveling in. And we're not just talking about lunches and beers here. These wide variances in costs between countries also usually occur with your accommodations, museum entrance fees, cab, bus and train fares, tours and just about any other costs that you encounter while traveling. And the longer your trip, the more these average daily costs will influence your total budget.

Now, this is not at all to say that you can never travel to more expensive places while on a tighter budget. As referenced in the previous "Introduction" section, we once spent a few weeks in New York City, one of the costliest cities in the world, and did it very inexpensively. But we did it using our methods outlined in this book, and very carefully planned out our activities (such as hitting museums on their free days) to make sure we didn't overspend. When we are traveling in an inexpensive country like Panama, or even a much less costly city in the U.S. such as Nashville or San Antonio, then we don't have to be nearly as careful about how often we eat in restaurants or which activities we decide to splurge on. And if we do need to stay in a hotel, it would not be as painfully expensive as New York City.

Now it's true that some places in the world offer things that are relatively unique, and some higher-cost destinations fall into this category. For instance, if you're really into theater, there aren't many other places in the world that can offer the enormous range of high quality theatrical performances that New York City or London do. Likewise for certain destinations and experiences that you can't have anywhere else, such as visiting the Galapagos Islands or going on safari in Africa – both fairly expensive trips. (*Note: We have done both these trips, and share ways to drastically cut costs even on such expensive destinations at our blog, HowtoTravelforFree.net. Just search for "Galapagos" or "safari!"*)

But this lack of another similar choice is certainly not always the case. Let's say that you really want to go to Switzerland because of the stunning natural beauty of its mountains. Well, the mountains in the Himalayan range of Nepal are just as striking, if not more so – can you say

Mount Everest? And Nepal is one of the cheapest countries in the world to visit, as opposed to Switzerland, which is one of the most expensive countries in the world to visit.

Likewise, there are other things to take into consideration besides costs within the countries themselves. For instance, if you're going to have to buy a really expensive plane ticket to get to somewhere like Nepal, then the total cost savings might not really be there. But then again, if you can get that same plane ticket for free by using airline points – BAM, you've got yourself a really inexpensive yet wonderful trip in the making.

Also, if you can only be gone for one week for your next trip, then traveling to the other side of the world may not make much sense, because you'd be spending such a large percentage of your time just getting there and back. These potential downfalls are part of what make traveling to Central America, one of the least expensive regions in the world, such a fantastic bargain for most Americans. The plane tickets, if you actually have to buy one, are usually not terribly costly, and the flights there don't take that long due to proximity.

Meals in inexpensive countries like Thailand are a fraction of the cost of meals in expensive places like Switzerland or Japan.

We find that there are also some non-monetary benefits to traveling in less expensive countries. For one, we often find them more interesting in a lot of ways. As much as we've enjoyed traveling in higher cost countries like Switzerland, Norway, Japan and Singapore, we find less expensive countries like Ecuador, El Salvador, India and Cambodia much more colorful and intriguing. Those cheaper countries tend to have cultures that are so much more different than our own that experiencing them tends to have more of an overall impact on our travel experience than traveling to wealthier, more globalized societies.

So in the big picture, while planning out your travels always keep these basic concepts in mind when trying to control your costs:

1. **You can either spend more money to get what you want quickly and more easily, or you can spend the time doing research and working different angles to get what you want for less money.**

2. **The longer you travel the less expensive your will be on an average daily basis, and the slower you travel the cheaper, and more meaningful, your trip is likely to be.**

3. **Which cities and countries you travel to greatly affects your total costs.**

"Twenty years from now you will be more disappointed by the things you didn't do than by the ones you did do. So throw off the bowlines, sail away from the safe harbor. Catch the trade winds in your sails. Explore. Dream. Discover." ~Mark Twain

TRANSPORTATION

AIRPLANES

Air travel is usually the main source of transportation, especially for international journeys, and it's typically the biggest expense of your trip. There is not much you can do about the fact that, in order to travel overseas, you will have to book flights that normally cost a lot of money. On top of that airlines have been raising prices on international flights in recent years, but there still are many tricks that can help you get the cheapest tickets possible and maximize your air travel dollars.

Frequent Flyer Miles
We typically save more money on our travel expenses than anything else by using frequent flyer miles to purchase our airline tickets. Think about the following example. Let's say we want to take a two-week trip to Cambodia and Laos, kind of like the one we took in 2012. If we were to use airline points to purchase our roundtrip airfare we'd be saving a minimum of $2400, and that's if we were to fly in low season. So for a two-week trip for two people we would be saving over $171 per day in total travel expenses (2400 ÷ 14). Unless you plan on staying at a really high-end hotel, it's going to be practically impossible for you to save more money on any other part of your trip.

So before you begin planning a big trip, it's vital that you research and organize your game plan for frequent flyer (FF) miles, and the earlier you start doing so the better. True, in the last few years the fees for redeeming these miles have gone up, while available dates and flights have gone down. But that doesn't mean that you can't still utilize them for significant amounts of free travel. This just means that you have to be up on the rules, know how to play the airlines' games, and be consistent about obtaining new frequent flyer miles with the right airlines.

I (Keith) haven't actually paid for a long international flight since 2009, and the only time I've paid for a domestic flight since then was when I found such a great price on a ticket that I saved my airline points for better usage elsewhere. And I've been taking two or three international trips a year for several years now. Bottom line: the amount of money that we've saved by using airline points for flights is truly incredible. Below are some examples:

- In June 2011 I used 25,000 miles total for a ticket from Austin to Seattle and a ticket from Vancouver, British Columbia back to Austin. The price for both of these one-way tickets together was about $500 at the time.
- In January 2012 I used a total of 130,000 miles for tickets for Shelley and me to fly from Austin to Cambodia (Shelley actually flew into Laos) and back. Using these miles saved us at least $3,300.
- In April 2012 we each used 80,000 miles to fly to and from Kenya. These tickets would have easily cost us around $1,500 or more per ticket.
- In July 2013 we used 120,000 points (total) for First Class tickets for a two-month trip to Latin America. We flew into Quito, Ecuador, and we returned to Austin from San Jose, Costa Rica. Because we flew First Class all of these tickets together would have cost us at least $4,000.

How To Travel Around The World For $418

In 2011 travel hacker Steve Kamb flew 35,000 miles in 12 months, visiting 15 cities, 9 countries and 4 continents for only 140,000 American Airlines points and $418 in fees – a set of flights that would normally have cost at least $6,000. And he acquired practically all of his airline points via credit card sign-up bonuses.

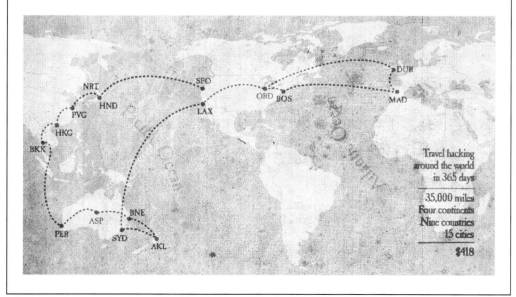

Travel hacking around the world in 365 days

35,000 miles
Four continents
Nine countries
15 cities

$418

The first step is to look at any existing plans and miles you already have, and the airlines that you may already fly with the most. If you have existing FF miles worth working with, you may want to stick with that program. If you don't, then you want to start by researching the major programs and choosing one or two. If you have a partner who often travels with you, you probably want to check with him or her as well for any programs they might have miles accrued in. When people travel together, it's much more advantageous for them to rack up miles in the same FF plan.

The major FF programs are alliances that include multiple airlines. Following is a list of the main alliances and the biggest airlines in them, but keep in mind that each alliance typically has several, perhaps dozens, of additional smaller airlines in its partnership program – as well as hotel and rental car chains. For up-to-date information on all major FF programs, including a success rating system and reviews, check out WebFlyer.com, or go to FrequentFlier.com for a complete list.

 The Three Largest Airline Partner Programs:

- OneWorld.com – American Airlines, British Airways, Cathay Pacific, Iberia, Japan Airlines, LAN, Qantas and others.
- SkyTeam.com – Delta, Air France, KLM, Alitalia, Air Europa, China Airlines, AeroMexico, Korean Air, Vietnam Airlines, Kenya Airways, etc.
- StarAlliance.com – United, US Airways, Air Canada, Lufthansa, Air New Zealand, ANA, Asiana, Austrian Airlines, EVA Air, SAS Scandinavian, Singapore Airlines, South African Airways, Swiss Air, TACA, Thai Airways and others.

Generally speaking, you want to take the following things into consideration when planning out how to best acquire airline points:

- **THIS IS VERY IMPORTANT. Be on the lookout for special promotional offers of large amounts of bonus frequent flyer miles for signing up for new credit cards and debit cards. These bonus offers let you rack up points incredibly fast – WAY faster than by solely using your credit cards that earn you miles for every day purchases and living expenses.** Getting points for every day expenses definitely helps, but we probably get about 95% of our points from these bonus miles offers. Because of this we try to sign up for 2-3 new credit cards with bonus miles every 3-4 months, with the goal of racking up at least 300,000 bonus points with various airlines every year. *(Please see more detailed information on credit card churning on page 28.)*

- Know which destinations you want to fly to the most and then figure out which airline partnerships cover the routes you would need to take.

- Try to spend your points wisely. Each airline has its own tier system for the amounts of points required for seats, and sometimes the mileage requirements are very different between different awards programs. Whether you fly coach or first class, try to get the seats that use the fewest amounts of points. Treat these points just like money, because in a way that's exactly what they are – the equivalent of travel dollars.

- If you have a flight problem like a big delay, cancellation, missed flight, rerouting or some combination thereof, make sure to complain the right way (2) to try to rake in mileage points. We have done this several times, including both of us getting reimbursed 35,000 miles each for our horrible journey (paid for with points in the first place!) to Nairobi, Kenya in 2012. If you have a bad flight experience make sure to keep as much of your flights' documentation as possible – this includes receipts and boarding passes. Then go to your airline's Customer Service page and make an online complaint. Be precise with details when describing the problem and specify how the problem affected you. Be assumptive in your tone that you expect compensation. Also copy your text and save it somewhere for potential use in the future before you hit the submit button. If you don't get a satisfactory response, then call into the customer service department to further plead your case. If you still don't get what you want then you can try using a Google search to find actual contact names and email addresses within the airline to send your complaint to. Throughout the entire process be cordial yet firm while keeping notes of your actions along the way.

- Review the ways in which you can receive FF mile credits; the major programs have many ways for earning credit besides flying on their airlines. You may find opportunities

Consider signing up with an airline point management website to keep up with your miles on different airlines. (see *Great Tools* below) They also give good information on how to accrue points faster through various offerings. Just don't let yourself use your precious earned points for non-travel related items!

such as banking, credit cards, cell phone or utility services that you would still use otherwise, that can accrue miles when used through their program.

- Be aware of which airlines you tend to fly the most often when you must pay for tickets. If you fly quite a bit with a particular airline and that airline is in partnership that covers the routes you are interested in, try to get additional points with that airline via credit card and debit card usages.

- Monitor the expiration dates of your miles. Each airline has different rules for this. Usually any activity on the account, no matter how big or small, will reset the expiration date further out.

Once you've selected and enrolled in your FF program of choice, it's important to review and know well the alliance airlines and other partners, and to utilize any of those services or products through your FF membership number in order to get full credit for everything. Sign up for the email newsletters that keep you informed about special offers and bonus miles, and keep abreast of program news. You can get miles by answering surveys, watching demos, dining out, shopping, etc.

You might be surprised, once you start traveling, how quickly enough miles for free tickets really can accrue. Personally, we participate in several of our FF programs' offerings such as dining club, online shopping, internet offerings such as banking or online movie memberships and credit cards, racking up miles for everyday expenses we would spent anyway. We use our airline credit cards for many normal purchases – particularly large ones – and then pay it off each month from our bank account.

We saved at least $3,500 on our RT flights to Cambodia & Laos by using frequent flier mile points.

Some monthly bills, perhaps a gym membership or cell phone service, can be automatically paid via a credit card. These can be great ways to accrue miles much faster with your everyday expenses, and we generate between 20 and 35 thousand miles annually this way – enough for a free domestic or international trip each year.

However, the important caveat with an airline miles credit card is to use it only for things you would be spending on anyway, and not make large purchases that you will have difficulty paying off quickly. Keep in mind that carrying a balance on these cards will incur interest and finance charges, and this can quickly offset any savings through FF awards. If you use the system of a FF program credit card, we highly recommend that you only use it if you pay off the balance each month with the money you would normally be paying for those purchases with, and not wasting your travel money on credit card balance fees. Played smart, frequent flyer programs are a great way to earn free trips.

Great tools for managing and using your frequent flyer miles:

- Points.com – A free online service that allows you to easily track and manage your different points programs. Be aware that trading and buying points here may not be such a great deal.
- TripIt.com – Another airline points management site that has strong mobile apps.
- MileageManager.com – An airline points manager that costs $14.95 per year but gives you more services.
- FlyerTalk.com – The MilesBuzz forum in the Miles & Points section is a great resource for up-to-date information on all the airline points programs.
- MillionMileSecrets.com – Another great resource for how to best accumulate and use miles with different airlines.
- ThePointsGuy.com – Has some great blog pieces with detailed information on how to use points for particular flights on specific airlines.
- FlightFox.com – For more complex routes it may be worth paying a small fee for experts to find the best deal for you.
- AwardGrabber.com – Find out when award seats will be released for your desired flight. It's usually 330 days before the flight, but this is not always the case. For the most coveted flights the award seats may only last a few minutes.

Credit Card Churning For Huge Airline Point Bonuses
There's a sub-culture of travelers out there who rack up hundreds of thousands of frequent flyer miles every year by signing up for several different credit cards that offer large chunks of bonus miles after hitting certain minimum spend requirements. It's called credit card churning, and I (Keith) have been doing this for years. I've accumulated well over a million miles so far, and I don't plan to stop any time soon. Why not fly all over the world for free? Below are some guidelines on how to do this.

- To apply for and keep applying for new cards you have to have a good credit score (perhaps 720 or better), and of course you have to maintain that good credit. If you don't have a good credit score now, build it back up first before applying for a new card. Always pay your bills on time, and try to keep your balances low. Each time you apply to a new card it dings your credit score around 2-5 points, but those hits go away in like 6-12 months. To get a free credit score update every month sign up for creditsesame.com. If you're planning to apply for a mortgage or other large loan soon, then hold off on applying for any new credit cards for the time being.

- Figure out which major airlines (and their partner airlines) you are likely to want to fly the most, and focus on getting cards that give large bonus points for those airlines. My personal experience is that Delta can be really hard to redeem miles with; Southwest, American and United tend to be easier, and US Airways and British Airways are kind of in the middle. The airline alliances you focus on will also greatly depend on the area of the world you want to travel to the most.

- I personally don't like offers for less than 25,000 bonus miles. I'd rather use my good credit, time and energy on bigger payoffs.

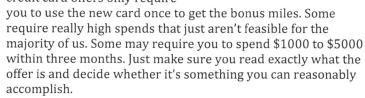

- Pay attention to the minimum spend requirements. Some credit card offers only require you to use the new card once to get the bonus miles. Some require really high spends that just aren't feasible for the majority of us. Some may require you to spend $1000 to $5000 within three months. Just make sure you read exactly what the offer is and decide whether it's something you can reasonably accomplish.

- Besides your normal expenses for things like buying groceries and gas and going to restaurants, you can often use your card to pay for insurance premiums, cell phone and internet services, car repairs, business travel and the like. For a small fee you can often pay for larger ticket items which will help you hit your spend requirements much faster. WilliamPaid.com lets you pay your rent online with a credit card. ChargeSmart.com enables you to pay your mortgage, auto loan, utility payments and other bills online with a credit card. You can also send money to a family member or friend via PayPal using a credit card and just have them reimburse you with a check. Usually these payment services sites charge around a 3% service fee. But these fees are completely worth it if the bonus miles you will get are large enough. Since I use my miles for international flights that are usually more costly, I figure every 10,000 miles I earn is worth about $200 to me. So, as an example, if I need to use these services to spend $3,000 on a credit card offer that will net me 50,000 points, then it will only cost me about $90 (.03 X 3,000) to get $1,000 worth of miles. That's a no-brainer.

- These frequent flyer credit cards almost always have annual fees associated with them, although often the first year's fee will be waived. If there is a first year fee, then decide whether it's worth it to you or not. A general rule I use is that if the annual fee is less than $100 and I can accumulate at least 30,000 miles with a reasonable spend requirement then it's worth it to me.

- If you are going to apply to multiple cards in a short amount of time it's best to do those applications on the same day, ideally on different browsers with the cookies deleted on each browser. If you want to spread those applications out, then try to wait at least 91 days in between application dates.

We saved $1,500 each by using points to fly to Africa in 2012.

Doing these things helps the credit card companies not see too many applications for credit in your name.

- If you get denied it often pays off to call the company to find out what the problem is. Sometimes something as simple as moving credit from another card will get your new card approved.

- I tend to keep my older credit cards that I've had for several years, because longer-term credit relationships strengthen your credit score. I tend to cancel more recently acquired credit cards before they are a year old. I don't want to pay the annual fee, and I want to be able to reapply for those same cards some day later.

- If you want to cancel and reapply for a certain card, know that there are different waiting periods for different companies. Generally speaking, from what I've seen recently, Bank of America and Barclays require you to wait six months after you cancel a card before you can apply to it again. American Express seems to require you to wait twelve months; Citi seems to require eighteen months; and Chase seems to require two years. These time requirements are always subject to change, and I try to keep abreast of the latest information on the Miles & Points section of flyertalk.com.

- Oftentimes a credit card offer will allow for a personal card as well as a business card, and it's very easy to show you have a business. It could be something as simple as selling a few items at home on eBay and claiming that as a small business.

- Sometimes a credit card offer will give you an additional 5,000 points just for adding someone else as a cardholder, perhaps a spouse or close friend. This person doesn't even have to be given the card when it arrives, so this can be a great way to accumulate even more points.

- It's a good idea to keep an updated document of some sort where you can keep all the dates you applied for which credit cards, the details of each offer (spend requirements, number of bonus miles, etc.), dates of cancelation, and other various notes that you deem important. If you end up churning a lot of cards, then having all of this information in one place will come in very handy as time goes on. Points.com and MileageManager.com are good websites to help you keep track of your accumulated miles with different airlines.

- Whenever you get a new card make sure to hit the spend requirements in the allotted time. You want to make sure you get those bonus points!

- Have fun with it! I treat credit card churning like a game. I enjoy winning this game by continuously getting more points with various airlines and then taking awesome trips all over the world with them.

Enjoying our favorite meal of our trip to Latin America in 2013 while in Cuenca, Ecuador — and as usual we used airline points to get there!

Traveling around the world is something I had planned to do when I was a little kid. When I turned 50, I sold everything I owned...my house, my car, my business, my furniture, my clothing...keeping fewer than 100 possessions that I could carry in a backpack. Over the next 3 years, I traveled to 38 countries...and by living frugally and simply, I was able to return "home" with enough money left over to give myself an additional year to decide what I want to be when I grow up!

It's a no-brainer that you should join the "One World Alliance" which allows you to accumulate frequent flyer miles from a number of different airlines. If you're traveling in a country where you're primarily using a local airline and don't think you'll be able to use the miles you're accumulating, you might consider trading those miles with someone who has surplus miles on an airline you will be using. Also, shop around and you can find credit card companies which offer rebates of up to 1.5% on all purchases.

--John Langford, CozmicCamera.com

"People don't take trips – trips take people."
~John Steinbeck

Finding The Best Airfares Without Using Airline Points

Although your first line of research for booking air tickets should be all the partner airlines in your frequent flyer alliance, there are times that you will need to or prefer to actually purchase your tickets instead. Perhaps you don't have enough points saved up yet to get a ticket using points. Or maybe the flights that you really need only have the higher tier airline point seats which typically require twice as many points as the lower tier seats, and you would rather use your miles more efficiently.

Read more tips and articles on working Frequent Flyer miles at our blog at howtotravelforfree.net. And, check out Keith's interview on the subject at The Washington Times (3).

Or, along the same vein, there might be a fare that is such a good deal that it makes more financial sense to save your points for another flight later. This is what happened to Keith for our trip to New York City in 2010 – he found a round-trip flight for less than $250 and decided to use those points for a much more expensive international flight at a later date.

Flexibility really is the key in getting the best prices on airfares. If you have to travel on specific dates, or during a destination's high season, you will almost certainly pay higher prices. Try to book as early as possible, several months in advance, to have the best luck. If your schedule allows it, look for off-season deals and be flexible on your travel times, and you will find the best deals.

When not booking during high season, oftentimes booking 6-8 weeks in advance can get you the best fare, and at the very least try to book your tickets at least 21 days before departure, often a requirement for many airlines to get their best rates. Also, several credible sources say that the best time of the week to purchase a ticket is after midnight Tuesday night (Wednesday morning) when the airlines' computer systems dump all of the unused reservations for sale-priced tickets that were make the previous weekend.

Make sure to compare the total price including all taxes and fees as you are looking at the different websites. Some sites are better at giving you this earlier in the online search process than others — Kayak, for example, always gives the total price including all taxes. The Kayak.com/explore/ and FareCompare.com/maps/ tools are terrific for searching prices for flights to destinations all over the world, on a map.

Sites we recommend to search for the best airfares:

- AirfareWatchdog.com
- BestFares.com
- CheapFlights.com
- FareCompare.com
- Globester.com
- Kayak.com
- MakeMyTrip.com
- Mobissimo.com
- Momondo.com
- Priceline.com
- SkyEurope.com
- SkyScanner.net
- WeGo.com
- Zoomtra.com

Another thing you can do is sign up for email newsletters from airlines and travel websites that will send you notices on specials and fare sales. Our favorite sites for searching for airfares are listed above – be sure to sign up for email notifications and sales alerts from them so you don't miss a deal!

Yet another good resource is Yapta.com, which stands for Your Amazing Personal Travel Assistant. Yapta alerts you when a particular fare price goes down. This can help you the most before you actually buy your ticket, but it can also help you afterwards. If you purchased your ticket directly from the airline and the price later goes down and if the price difference is more than the rebooking fees involved you can get refunded with a travel voucher for future use. For higher priced tickets, especially those for longer international routes, the savings can be significant. And for a $15 fee Yapta will even do the legwork for you.

There are also the major travel search and booking sites. Although they often don't include low-cost airlines (see more on low-cost airlines below), they are worth checking out and mainly, signing up to receive fare alert newsletters. However, we personally prefer the sites listed on the previous page, for finding the absolute best fares on all airlines.

- Expedia.com
- Hotwire.com
- Orbitz.com
- Travelocity.com

Once you have found a great airfare on an aggregator or booking site, you should also go to the airline's website to check the fare directly before purchasing the ticket. Occasionally it will be lower. You could even take it a step further and do a search on Google.com for 'promotion codes' along with the name of the airline. If you are lucky you might find a code that fits your itinerary and can be used on the airline's website for an additional discount.

Lastly, when booking airfare on any airline and trying to find the best deal, don't overlook "Hidden City" and "Throwaway Ticketing" options. This is a really interesting take on a creative way to save potentially big money when booking flights. Often, the quoted airfare to the city you want to fly to may be WAY higher than a flight to a different city, but with a connection IN your destination city. By booking a different flight through your destination (and just not taking that second leg), you can sometimes save big money.

Here's an example: A nonstop one-way ticket from Des Moines to Dallas/Fort Worth is $375 on American Airlines, for example. But a ticket from Des Moines to Los Angeles – with a layover in Dallas – is only $186. You book that ticket, get off in Dallas and don't take the second leg into LA.

Shelley has actually done this before. Another example of this is when you need a one-way flight, but the round-trip flights are MUCH cheaper. It is often better to book the RT flight, and just not take the return flight. Just make sure that you book the FIRST flight as the one you actually want to fly, because usually if you don't show up to take the first flight of your ticket, the airline will cancel the whole thing.

There's more information and examples at <u>this article on BoardingArea.com</u> (4).

Low Cost Airlines
After checking with the aggregators and the airlines that the aggregators mention then it's always best to see if the aggregator searches didn't include a budget airline flight. Some budget airlines do not allow themselves to be listed with aggregators - Southwest Airlines is a perfect example. And there are times when the many no-frills, low-cost airlines present deals too good to pass up. Below is a list of the main low-cost airlines in North America.

The main low-cost airlines in North America are:

- <u>Air Tran</u>
- <u>Allegiant Air</u>
- <u>Frontier</u>
- <u>Horizon/Alaska Air</u>
- <u>Jet Blue</u>
- <u>Mesa Air</u>
- <u>Spirit</u>
- <u>Southwest</u>
- <u>Sun Country</u>
- <u>Virgin America</u>
- <u>WestJet</u>

Budget airlines can be especially helpful in finding a cheaper airfare outside of the US. In other parts of the world there are even more low-cost airlines, some with ridiculously low fares. Most notably, these are in Europe and Asia. The famed and ever-popular <u>Ryan Air</u>, based in the U.K., offers incredible fares, sometimes as low as one Euro, plus airport taxes. Shelley flew from Prague to Milan for $25 US, and from Paris to Barcelona for $40. The best deals are to and from destinations in the U.K. <u>EasyJet</u> is another very popular European airline offering extremely cheap fares. Try <u>TACA</u> in Mexico and Central America, <u>JetStar</u> in Australia. We have both taken several flights for merely the cost of airport taxes with specials from <u>Air Asia</u>, a low-cost Asian airline based out of Malaysia. <u>Tiger Airways</u> is another good option to check out for Asia.

Africa and South America seem to present the most difficulty in finding cheap tickets and airlines that serve the whole continent; although if you are traveling *to* these destinations *from* Europe or North America, you may have better luck. For example, LAN is known for their reasonable fares between the U.S. and South American destinations.

There are some signs that airline competition may be opening up on these continents, however. For example, Africa's first budget airline, FastJet, recently started doing business based out of Tanzania.

Unfortunately, Whichbudget.com is no longer a good resource for finding out which budget airlines fly on the routes that you need around the world. A good place to start is Wikipedia's "List of low-cost airlines" (5), but it's not complete. If you don't find a budget airline for a country or connection that you are looking for in this list, you might try asking a question about it on Lonely Planet's online Thorn Tree Forum (6).

Do keep in mind though, that if you are going to be traveling slowly and over a long period of time, it's often better to buy domestic airline tickets *in* the country when you're there, rather than beforehand. This is especially true in Africa and parts of Asia, where online booking with a credit card outside the country can be difficult due to high levels of internet fraud. Also keep in mind that many low-cost airlines operate from smaller, outlying airports. Because of this, you will often sacrifice the convenience of landing at a major, big-city airport to fly

on the cheap, and you may have to take a bus into the city from an outlying area that is 30 minutes or more away.

One very strong rule to remember when flying on any low-cost airline is this:

Carefully read the rules and fine print!

As with virtually all airlines these days, the low-cost carriers have many rules that, if not noted and adhered to, can cost you dearly and offset your savings. These airlines operate on slim margins, and offer their extremely cheap fares for the basic flight – and nothing more. Typically you will have to pay for any checked baggage, and any beverages or food during the flight. What's more, if you indicate at booking that you have no checked baggage, but show up at the airport with a bag to check, you may pay more (possibly twice as much!) than you would have online, ahead of time. Also pay close attention to weight restrictions for checked baggage; going over can be really expensive. Be sure to thoroughly review all the rules – some low-cost airlines even charge you if you do not check in online. Knowing what to expect and taking the time to learn it will avoid losing your fare savings in hefty fees.

All in all, finding a budget airline flight can sometimes save you a ton of money, especially for international flights, so it's definitely be worth the effort to research them in your quest to find the best overall deal.

Air Consolidators
Consolidators purchase tickets, mostly international, in bulk at wholesale prices directly from the airlines and then resell them for a profit but often at a much lower price than the airline's published fares. The United States Air Consolidators Association (USACA.com), American Society of Travel Agents (ASTA.org), International Air Transport Association (IATA.org), and United States Tour Operators Association (USTOA.com) are professional organizations that require certain standards be met for membership. These are good places to start looking for a great fare.

Other great places to find consolidators are in ethnic communities whose travel agencies often specialize in tickets to the countries that many in the community came from. Just make sure that the organization is legitimate by at least checking with the Better Business Bureau and with any professional travel organizations that it claims to be a part of. Likewise, be aware of what the restrictions are. For instance some consolidator fares don't allow frequent flier miles to accrue, and some have severe penalties for changes or cancelations. Always ask. Lastly, try to use a major credit card to make your purchase. If by chance there is a problem with the ticket this will give you some recourse by asking your credit card company to deny payment.

Air Travel Checklist:

When planning air travel, plan well in advance for the best fares and availability, and always check your tickets before leaving your travel agency to make sure all the information is correct. In addition, ask the following questions prior to booking your reservations:

- What restrictions apply to the tickets?
- Is this a direct flight, or will I have to change planes, terminals, or have a layover?
- How and when do I obtain seat assignments and boarding passes?
- What type of payment can I use?
- How and when should I reconfirm my flights?
- What are the size and weight restrictions, and number of pieces of luggage allowed?
- What type of insurance should I purchase?
- How do I make special requests for my flight reservations, such as special meals/diet, aisle or window seats, assistance to the gate?
- Will I get credit for my frequent flyer program?
- What documentation is necessary for this flight?
- Is this a code-share flight?

TRAINS

In some places of the world, traveling by train can often be more expensive than flying, due to the proliferation of low-cost airlines as we have just explored in the previous section. We have often been shocked to research transportation costs between, for example, two European capitals only to find that we can fly on a low-cost airline for $20-50, when the same train route would cost between $200 and $300!

Even in places like India, where train travel has traditionally been very cheap, the explosion of new airlines over the past few years means that it is often almost as cheap to fly. Often the decision to go by plane or train depends on where in the world you are traveling, and then comparing the costs as well as the time involved. On a recent trip to India, for example, I (Shelley) compared traveling between Mumbai and Goa on the train or flying. The cost of a second-class air-conditioned train ticket was about $25, and the round-trip airfare was $60. However, the flight took less than two hours and the train trip was almost 24 hours. I chose to fly. Many other times and places in India, however, I have taken the train –

even overnight trains – particularly when the airfare was much more expensive or the destinations were not large cities with major airports.

Trains can often be a better bet if your distance is short. With the hassle and extra time and security involved with flying these days, train travel is typically less stressful and much more comfortable. Compared to an actual flight time of one to two hours, for example, in most places you can take a six hour train trip in almost the same total amount of time, allowing for the extra one to two hours ahead of time you arrive at the airport, waiting for baggage claim, etc. Many people in the US don't even consider train travel, when Amtrak has an excellent rail system and nice railway cars. For many short distances (six hours or less) between metropolitan areas, Amtrak can be far cheaper than flying, much less hassle, depart and arrive in city centers rather than outlying airports, and offer greater comfort.

Traveling by rail can be the way to go if you need flexibility; rather than airline tickets that incur hefty fees for any changes once purchased, rail passes are generally hop-on types of things (although reservations at least the day before are usually required), and changes or last-minute purchases do not cost extra, for the most part. Trains also make sense if you are doing a lot of traveling within one country or region that offers a rail pass, such as the popular Rail Europe Pass that can be used over weeks or months in dozens of European countries. Train tickets can also often be cheaper if they are purchased in the country where you're traveling, from a local agent or website, rather than online from your home country ahead of time. However, this is not *always* the case – a Eurail pass for example. Be sure to check ahead of time.

Riding the "Devil's Nose" train in Ecuador, July 2013

And of course, another big advantage that rail travel has over flying is that it does not result in the huge carbon emissions that airplane travel does, and is much more environmentally friendly. It also provides a great opportunity to meet and get to know locals, oftentimes sharing food, drinks and life stories along the way.

- Seat61.com – The best website for train travel information
- AmTrak.com
- Irctc.co.in
- RailEurope.com
- RailPass.com
- TrainTraveling.com

Don't forget to utilize train systems within a metropolitan area once you arrive – most major cities throughout the world have excellent train or subway systems that can provide the most efficient and cheapest way to get around a city.

> *"The open road is a beckoning, a strangeness,*
> *a place where a man can lose himself."*
> *~William Least Heat Moon*

CARS

With the high cost of gas and the time it takes to drive places, travel by automobile is usually not the preferred method except for shorter trips. However, within a relatively small geographic area, driving can make sense and save money – particularly if you are traveling with several people. Splitting the cost of gas, tolls or parking, and possible car rental fees between three or four people is often cheaper than flights or trains, and of course offers a flexibility that can't be matched with mass transit. With a car, you can go where you want to go and stay however long you like, without being bound by airport and railway station locations or timetables. There are also more remote, rural places all over the world that are simply not accessible by any other way than driving. We found this to be the case on a recent trip to El Salvador.

For bidding sites such as Priceline, you can see what bids people are winning with at biddingfortravel.com. At these sites it's usually more advantageous to start with a very low price – you would be surprised at what bids will get accepted. I (Shelley) rented a car for two weeks in Hawaii, generally one of the most expensive places to rent a car, for $12 per day using Priceline. However, keep in mind that if your bid is not accepted then you must wait 24 hours to bid again unless you change one of three things – car size, dates or location.

Some good websites for finding the best rental car deals are:

- AutoEurope.com
- BreezeNet.com (owned by Priceline – good for non-US rentals)
- CarRentalExpress.com
- CarRentals.com
- Europe by Car
- Hotwire.com
- Orbitz.com
- Priceline.com
- RentalCars.com (owned by Priceline – same results, different format)

The earlier you reserve a rental car the better, especially if you will be traveling in high season. And if you can cancel a reservation without a penalty then it makes even more sense to make a reservation early, then just cancel it later if you end up finding a better deal. Weekend rates typically start on Thursday at noon, and they are often significantly less expensive than the weekday rates. Weekly rates are typically based on rentals for 5-7 consecutive days and are almost always a much better value. However, be aware that if you turn in your car before you hit the weekly time threshold, you might get charged the higher daily rate. Also, compare rates for different types of cars – the smaller compact cars are not always the least expensive.

Compare rates for different pick up locations whenever you have that kind of flexibility. For instance, it is usually more expensive to rent a car from a location within an airport due to additional taxes and fees, although this is not always the case, especially when it comes to highly densely populated cities like New York where space is a premium. Likewise, different locations for the same rental company within the same city can vary quite a bit in prices for the same types of cars. Do keep in mind hours of operation though – for instance some locations have limited opening hours on weekends.

Here are some additional tips on renting cars:

- Enterprise offers free pick up and drop off services within 10 miles of the rental office. This could enable you to not have to get a rental car the day you arrive at the airport, thereby shaving off a day's rental and potential parking costs. Likewise, you wouldn't be paying the typically higher in-airport rates, and you wouldn't need to pay for transportation from your hotel to pick up and drop off your car.

- When comparing quotes from different websites make sure all the taxes and fees are included for each quote. Some websites are better than others at revealing this information more transparently. Likewise, take into account the total cost if you will be adding extra items such as additional drivers, a GPS navigation device, insurance, etc. Pricing on these items can vary substantially between rental companies.

- When you pick up the car do not opt for the prepaid gas service with the rental company unless you know for sure that you will return the car close to empty, or you will end up paying for gas you didn't use. Likewise, don't forget to fill up the tank just before you return the car or you will pay dearly for the rental company to do it for you.

- Pay attention to the rules and rates for mileage. Many rentals now come with unlimited mileage, but this is not always the case. And if it does come with unlimited mileage you are usually required to stay within a certain geographic area, such as the same state. Some cars even have GPS devices on them to help enforce this.

- If you will need to cross an international border make sure that it is allowed within your rental contract and that you have the appropriate paperwork with you, including proof of insurance.

- Be careful about using a debit card when reserving or paying for a car. First of all, if you are counting on insurance coverage from a credit card with which you made the reservation, this would then nullify that coverage. Also, rental companies often put an authorization hold of up to $500 on the card, which could freeze up those funds in your bank account for up to two weeks after you turn the car back in – potentially a big problem if you are counting on having access to that cash.

Another great innovation in the short-term car rental business is companies like ZipCar and Car2Go. Sometimes you may not need to rent a car for your entire stay, or even for days at a time. Particularly if you are in a metropolitan area near the center of town, don't have easy access to efficient public transportation, and don't need constant access to a car for multiple days in a row which may make renting a car more economical, then these short-term car usage companies could be the least expensive way to go.

Zipcar.com is actually an auto-sharing program rather than a car rental company. ZipCar has a $25 one time application fee as well as a $50 annual fee, and then it costs just $7+ per hour or $69+ per day to use the cars. Gas, insurance, up to 180 miles of usage and free parking at ZipCar sites are included – a huge advantage if you are going to be in a city where parking is expensive and difficult to find. Members can pick cars up anytime after reserving them online or on the phone. Look on their website for the current list of covered cities in the US, Canada and the UK, as well as exact mapped locations of all their cars in real time on their websites. Car2Go is a similar program, with parking sites all over the metropolitan areas they operate in. This can also result in big savings on parking fees when in a dense urban downtown area. Also, check out CarSharing.net, which provides a pretty comprehensive list of car share organizations, including these as well as many others, in cities across the US.

You might also consult AutoDriveaway.com, a service that helps people move their cars when they don't want to drive themselves or pay for shipping. As a driveway volunteer, you get a "rental" car, plus your first tank of gas, for free. If you're over 21, just fill out an application form, present a valid driver's license and references, and pay a $350 refundable deposit (though sometimes they may require fingerprinting or a driving history from the DMV), and take off down the road. You pay for the rest of the gas as well as lodging for your trip.

One other aspect of driving as your method of transportation that we should mention here, is RVing. Many long-term travelers use an RV as both their means of transportation and accommodations. In fact, some very good friends of ours, Greg and Angie Rose, recently returned home from nearly two years of traveling the United

States in their camper van — along with their dog, Kipper. All the details about how they did it are in a story on our blog (8).

And WandrlyMagazine.com has a great, detailed piece from another couple who have been living on the road in an RV with their children. They claim that living on the road can be quite a bit cheaper than living in a fixed location — and they show the complete financial breakdown to help illustrate how to make it happen, including costs in different locations around the United States.

Ride Sharing

Sharing a ride is a popular cheap travel option, especially among the backpacker type crowd. With ride sharing, two or more travelers who are going to the same place, split the cost of gas and other travel expenses to travel together. Often the person who owns the vehicle will contribute the auto and ride, and other travelers will cover the gas and travel expenses.

 Several websites exist to post and search listings that will connect potential ride share partners:

- Erideshare.com
- Craigslist.com
- KindRideShare.org
- Rideshare-Directory.com
- Ridester.com
- GoLoco.org
- CarpoolWorld.com
- Gishigo.com
- Gumtree.com.au

Of course, sharing a ride can be set up on a much more personal, informal basis by using traditional networking methods and asking friends and people you know. While traveling, more communal places like hostels, where travelers get to know each other and share resources, are often a good place to partner up for ride sharing and traveling buddies.

Check out Tripping.com, a global travel hosting community for rideshares as well as homestays, meeting locals for coffee or meals, and travel tips!

One of the most important things that can be said about this option, perhaps obviously, is that safety and caution are of utmost importance. Be extremely careful about who you set up a ride or travel arrangements with, exercise due diligence, make sure that several other people know of your plans and exact itinerary, and above all, listen to your instincts if they tell you something isn't quite right.

Erideshare.com offers these safety tips:

- All eRideShare members correspond by anonymous email. You send your message using a form on the site, using your eRideShare member ID, and it is forwarded to their regular address. They correspond with you in the same way. Your email address and identification remain private.
- You should meet the person you're considering traveling with, in a public place, before agreeing to travel together. Discuss driving safety.
- Confirm your prospective travel partner's phone number by calling it. Other ways of increasing confidence include exchanging photographs, copying your travel partner's driver's license or other photo ID information, and asking for personal references and calling them.
- We suggest that you exchange emergency contact numbers before traveling, and exchange any important medical information.

BUS LINES

Buses are often one of the most economical ways to travel; although again correlating with our rule of time versus money, they generally take the longest time to get anywhere. Even at home in the U.S., we are fans — for example, MegaBus can be cheaper than driving, with special fares as low as $1!

There are many different types of buses that you may take advantage of, depending on where you are and your travel purposes. There are large interstate and inter-country bus systems such as Greyhound; there are also tour buses run by travel operators, which can offer both package tour deals as well as a la carte tickets for bus transport only.

BusStation.net is probably the best website for information on bus travel throughout the entire world. GotoBus.com sells bus tickets and bus travel packages for several US destinations.

Within a region or country, local commuter or cross-country buses can provide an extremely inexpensive way to travel. For example, in Costa Rica if you want to go from San Jose to Monteverde, you can pay a minimum of $35 for a tourist bus (depending on the number of passengers) – or $5 for the regular public bus. An excellent destination travel rule to remember is:

Find out what the locals do – it's usually the most convenient and least expensive.

Although we are particularly talking here about transportation, this is true for virtually every aspect of travel, from where to eat to what to see. When it comes to transportation, many visitors automatically look at the tourist options only, from travel guidebooks, visitor centers or tour agents. But if you find out how the locals travel and what the local options are, you will often find the cheapest way to get somewhere.

Again, this may take a little more time. A tour or Greyhound-style bus will most often go directly from point A to point B; a local commuter bus, on the other hand, may very well have many stops in between. The cost savings, however, can be so significant as to offset this for most budget travelers.

Another thing to consider when using local modes of transport is that they are, well...local. Meaning that they will speak the local language, and depending on where you are, possibly not even speak English; the transport will be full of the color and everyday business of life. Somewhere in rural South America, you may be sharing the bus with chickens or pigs. In coastal Africa it could be the day's fishing haul. An exasperated mother may ask you to hold her child, and other passengers may be fascinated with you and play Twenty Questions about your life and what you are doing there. In this writer's opinion, of course, this is all part of the fun and adventure, and simply adds to the appeal of such travel. Going locally means that you will likely meet people and have experiences that you would never get the chance to have on a tour bus filled with other visitors.

BOATS/FERRIES

Clearly, water travel options will largely depend on the geographical region of the world you are in. Ferry travel is much more popular in Europe and some parts of Asia, for example; although regions of the US, such as the Pacific Northwest, the Massachusetts coast and the Florida Keys where there are many islands, ferry and boat travel is prevalent.

The cost of traveling by ferry or boat, compared to other options such as flying, is largely dependent on the availability of other options. In some cases, ticket prices for a ferry may be just as expensive or more so than flying or driving might be. In other circumstances, you may find that traveling by boat takes longer, but is much cheaper.

The International Ferry Directory (9) lists all ferry lines throughout the world, and is a good place to start. Keep water travel in mind as an option at least worth checking out and pricing, when you are traveling in areas widely spread across islands and bodies of water. Some of the most popular regions of the world for ferry travel are:

Pacific Northwest, USA	Spain/Morocco
British Columbia & Alaska	United Kingdom/English Channel
Eastern Seaboard, USA	Southern Europe (Croatia, Italy)
Scandinavia	Japan/Philippines
Greece & Turkey	Hong Kong

One word of caution: According to a report in the Washington Times (10), ferries in the developing world are one of the least safe modes of transportation. The Times stated that massive overcrowding and poor regulations often contribute to ferry accidents, reiterating that the danger lies in poor countries, largely in Southeast Asia where water travel is heavily relied on and resources are few.

BICYCLYING

Traveling by bike has multiple advantages. It's one of most inexpensive modes of transportation, as well as extremely healthy and environmentally friendly. Not only that, but because bicycling automatically puts you into the slow method of travel (like walking), you will likely see more, meet more locals, and have a much deeper travel experience. Traveling by bicycle, especially combined with camping or staying in hostels, is one of the absolutely cheapest ways to travel; in fact, you could probably travel across an entire continent for six months this way, for the amount of money a typical two-week vacation might cost with airfare and fancy hotel – without a fraction of the experiences, cultural interactions and adventures.

Clearly, biking your way around requires a certain amount of physical strength and stamina, and is not for everyone. And for those who do travel by bike, it doesn't necessarily make up the single or majority mode of transportation. Deciding when, where and for how long you are going to bicycle completely depends on your fortitude and how much time you have. Traveling by bike is much more common in some parts of the world, particularly Europe and many Asian countries. It is also quite popular among certain travelers, so that there are companies who do nothing but organize bicycle tours.

Of course, traveling with a tour company and purchasing their packages will be much more expensive than independent bike travel. However, if you are really new to either cycling or travel – much less both – it might be a good way to begin. You could start with just a short bike tour with an operator, to gain experience and make sure it's something that you not only like to do, but can do. This will give you a good basis later on for planning and executing your own bike travels independently, and saving

Check out a great post by our friends at BootsnAll Travel on Budget Travel by Bike: How You Can Do It for $14 per Day! (11).

a lot of money in the process. There are even a few bicycle hospitality groups, through which you can meet up with other bikers all over the world, sometimes even staying with them in homestay accommodations. Check out WarmShowers.org and the BikeFriday.com/community/.

Depending on the total length of your travels and how much cycling fits into them, there are several options for traveling with a bicycle. If you plan to travel mostly by bike, you can take your bicycle with you. Most airlines let you check a bicycle (albeit for a fee, sometimes hefty, so research heavily!) and you can almost always take it on a train or boat as well. There are also folding bikes such as the Brompton and Bike Friday (mentioned previously), that can even be packed into a suitcase and provide a much easier method of transporting the bike when you are incorporating it into air travel and larger travel plans.

Another option, particularly when bicycling will be one mode of transportation or one leg of travel among many, is to rent a bicycle. Bike rentals are generally available the world over, although if you want to ride from point A to point B – in other words, one way travel where you leave the bike in a different place from where you started – options become more narrow. Start with doing an internet search for bike rental in the city or country you will be visiting, and also ask the local visitors center, tourist bureau or hotel concierge. One possibility you might consider is purchasing a bike, particularly a used one, and then selling it when you are done with your bicycle tour.

Clearly, one of the limitations of bike travel, like backpacking, is baggage. You can only carry so much on your person and on your bike, and this mode of travel forces you to pack light. However, most long-term and world travelers see this as an advantage, and you may very well come to feel that way, too. For both of us – along with most other extensive travelers – the
more and longer we have traveled in our lives, the less we pack and less we are willing to lug around with us, no matter what our mode of transportation may be. It's far easier to carry minimal equipment and a few changes of clothing and wash every few days; and lightening up your load really enables you to be flexible, move around, and jump on travel adventures in ways that someone with a four-piece luggage set can never do.

Don't think that biking has to only be considered for long distances or traveling between locations. Even if that isn't for you, lots of major cities have bike rental or share programs, particularly in North America and Europe. Paris (12) was one of the early innovators of this, and their sleek silver bikes can be found at street corners all over the city, with kiosks for completing the rentals. Japan and China were also pioneers of the city-wide public bicycle program. We have rented bikes to get around in Laos,

Chile and Puerto Rico, to name a few. Read this article at <u>TreeHugger.com</u> (13) for details on public bike projects around the globe.

Don't be intimidated by the thought of traveling by bicycle; such a trip only has to be as strenuous as you make it. As Friedel Grant, who has pedaled 48,000 km through 30 countries with her husband, points out, "Don't fancy camping every night and crossing continents at a racing pace? Go instead for a laid-back ride along Europe's canal and riverside paths—no traffic and flat—or a jaunt through New Zealand's vineyards, stopping at a B&B each night." Other advice includes training at home beforehand, and starting modestly. Their excellent website full of ideas and advice is <u>TravellingTwo.com</u>.

For more inspiration check out the blog of Tim Travis, an American who saved money, sold his possessions, quit his job and began traveling the world by bicycle. This was in 2002, and he is still on the road. You can read about Tim's adventures and glean a lot of great bicycle travel tips at <u>downtheroad.org</u>.

Our list of good websites for bicycle tours and travel:

- <u>CyclingHolidays.org</u>
- <u>AdventureCycling.org</u>
- <u>BicycleTour.com</u>
- <u>Backroads.com</u>
- <u>EscapeAdventures.com</u>
- <u>BicycleTouringPro.com</u>
- <u>BicyclingWorld.com</u>
- <u>Bike-Sharing.blogspot.com</u>

"Do not follow where the path may lead. Go instead where there is no path and leave a trail." ~Ralph Waldo Emerson

WALKING

Like biking, transporting yourself around with your own two feet is a cheap, healthy and eco-conscious way to travel. Walking is slower than bike travel, although less cumbersome and generally easier to plan; and like biking, many tour companies have sprung up that offer walking trips. The company <u>BackRoads.com</u>, mentioned above in the bicycle section, offers walking tours as well as biking ones. Some others are:

- WalkingAdventures.com
- WebWalking.com
- WalkingConnection.com

Some people are concerned that by walking, they will see less because they might not always be able to get to the top 20 tourist spots recommended in the guidebook, in the amount of time they have in a place. In fact, by seeing less you will see more. Our personal feeling is that perhaps you don't *want* to see the top 20 tourist spots; maybe by choosing only the handful that really appeal to you, then you will be able to see more of this place you have traveled to, *in between* the sightseeing destinations. This is where real life is lived, after all. Walking forces you out of the confining tourist bubbles designed for foreigners, and allows you to experience local patterns of life that may be intriguingly different from your own. People coming home from work, stopping at the market, and walking with their children or pets.

You will also likely stumble upon the best places to eat, by trying a place that is bustling, but only with locals. Chances are these markets and restaurants are by far much less expensive, and higher quality, than the ones on the tourist trail that are geared, after all, to tourists. We have had some of the best meals of our lives this way, and not always in exotic spots. Even wandering aimlessly around the Village in New York, for example, Shelley and her mother found a tiny neighborhood lunch spot run by a Greek family, with about eight tables clearly full of local regulars. One of our good friends met a guy in Barcelona, by getting lost and stopping at a busy neighborhood restaurant by herself. She ended up invited to dine at the next table over with him and his friends, which gave her not only a chance to practice her Spanish and meet the locals, but the start of a love affair.

Also, in some places of the world, you can really only see what you want to see, what is magnificent to witness, on foot. Many of mankind's greatest achievements are best explored under your own power. Hidden in the mountains of Peru, Machu Picchu can only be explored by wandering over its ancient stone steps and through its amazing stone architecture. Likewise, China's Great Wall offers an incomparable walking experience, especially if you seek out the wild, unrestored sections that are well away from the access points where busloads of tourists are dropped off each morning.

Here are a few good free walking tour companies:

- imfree.com.au (Australia)
- BigAppleGreeters.org (NYC)
- athensfreewalkingtour.com
- guided-brasov.com
- befreetours.com (Bratislava)
- NewEuropeTours.eu (Europe)

Many cities in the world have organizations that offer free walking tours – which is not only healthy for the travel budget, but are great ways to learn about the place you've just landed. 90% of the major European cities offer this, as well as many large cities in Asia, Australia, New Zealand and the U.S.

Besides being free, and good for you, walking has a huge added advantage in a realm that most travelers prize highly: photography. Being on foot allows you to see photo opportunities you never would otherwise, and unique angles that capture the real soul of a place. Face it, whether we've been there or not, we've all seen photos of the Coliseum in Rome and the beach in Rio. What we haven't seen is the Italian mother hanging her laundry out the window a few blocks away, or the children you came across playing in the alleys of the favelas in Brazil.

HITCHHIKING

Like ride sharing and couch surfing, hitchhiking can be a mode of travel that will get you around a lot of places for free or very cheaply. However, it goes without saying that extreme caution must be taken not only when hitchhiking, but when deciding where to do so. We include this as a free travel method because we have a number of adventurous friends who have done it often with no problems or qualms; in fact, it has become part of their best travel stories and how they have met some friends all over the world. Most of these people are men, we should point out, or they hitchhiked in pairs or groups. It's a possibly viable alternative, but we include it with full disclosure that it's probably not a good idea for one or two women traveling alone, and for all travelers to exercise caution when thinking about it.

That being said, some places in the world are very open and safe for hitchhiking; in fact, it is a common and accepted practice. In Cuba, for instance, the majority of the populace do not own cars and not only is hitchhiking a daily routine of life, but drivers are expected to stop and offer a ride to people on their route who are waiting on the side of the road. The practice is even encouraged by the government as a way of meeting shortages and overcrowding on buses and trains in the country.

Even where it's not as typical of a practice among locals, there are many places where hitchhiking is common among traveling visitors, and the locals are comfortable with it and willing to lend a hospitable hand. Hitchhiking by traveling backpackers is relatively common in Australia, New Zealand, Canada and Europe (though less so in France and Spain). Some of the most difficult countries are in South America; Bolivia and Argentina are known to be nearly impossible. Another thing to be aware of is that hitchhiking customs vary around the world.

While in most Western countries sticking your thumb out is standard, in Latin America it's more of a wrist flip. In Southeast Asia the gesture is a hand-wave-down motion, and in other places you point at the ground. Also, be sure to find out if hitchhiking is even legal in the country where you are, before you attempt it; in some places it is strongly discouraged and even illegal, and violators can be fined. For a resource and tips, you might want to check out DigiHitch.com.

Checklist of Documents to Take on your Trip:

_____**Airline Tickets:** If you were issued paper tickets, you *must* have them with you. Printouts of e-tickets and reservations are a good idea.

_____**Confirmation Numbers:** Having confirmation documentation will help straighten things out if you can't find your reservation at the ticket kiosk or at the hotel desk. This applies for airline flights, hotel reservations, tours, rental cars, even ferries and trains.

_____**Itinerary:** A paper copy of your itinerary will let help ensure you are getting what you paid for.

_____**Vouchers:** If you're taking a tour, you may receive vouchers in the mail for hotels, transfers and different parts of the tour. Take them with you.

_____**Contact Numbers:** Make sure you have local phone numbers for contacts or tour agencies you're using; as well as emergency numbers for your credit cards and banks, and family/friends back home.

_____**Photo Copies:** Make good photo copies of your passport and birth certificate to take with you. If you ever lose your passport or have it stolen, this will make it much easier to replace.

_____**Extra Passport Photos:** Take extra passport size photos, for international travel. If you need to apply for a visa upon entry, you may need one or two.

Brainstorm Session – Alternative Travel Options:

ACCOMMODATIONS

If you've ever traveled on a shoestring (or on no string at all), you're probably well aware of the many places where you can stay on the cheap. But there are also many places where you can stay for free!

In this section, we will give an overview and description of the different types of lodging available, to start the ideas flowing and let you begin thinking about the style of accommodations that suit you best – as well as others you may not have thought about. We will also highlight the many different ways in which you can stay at these accommodations for free, or next to nothing. The next chapter, **Creative Ways to Travel**, will explore in far more detail some of the methods mentioned in this chapter as well. The various types of accommodations are listed here in general ascending order of cost, beginning with those that are most likely to be completely free and ending with the most expensive options.

HOME EXCHANGE

This is one of **our absolute favorite ways to travel**, and the method by which we have done the vast majority of traveling for free. But our love of home exchanging goes beyond the monetary. Based on our personal experiences only, there are not enough positive things to be said about home exchanging as a way not only to receive accommodations at absolutely no cost, but to also save money in many other ways and greatly broaden the entire travel experience.

I (Shelley) got involved with home exchanging after reading an article about it nearly a decade ago. After doing a little research and browsing other home exchange listings, I signed up at HomeExchange.com and input all the details about my house. I was heading to Prague the summer of 2007, to attend a writing program for a month, and I thought it would be great if I could find a

Shelley's beautiful home exchange casita in San Miguel de Allende, Mexico – January 2013

57

home exchange for that period. While I didn't find anything in the Czech Republic (and ended up renting an apartment instead), I did find several other exchanges in European cities that I traveled to for several weeks after my Prague program was over.

My first exchange was in Paris; I contacted and began communicating with a very sweet young professional named Sophie. She traveled a lot for her job, and she and her boyfriend had never been to Prague and were very interested in doing so. After numerous emails, we worked out an exchange agreement whereby she and her boyfriend would come stay in the apartment I had rented in Prague one weekend (while I was gone visiting another town through my writing program); and I would stay in her Paris flat for over a week. Her apartment turned out to be an absolutely charming, small one bedroom in the heart of Le Marais – an exceptional location.

Read Shelley's interview about home exchanging with The Washington Times (14).

My first exchange illustrated one of the common aspects of home exchanges – you don't have to do a completely equal or simultaneous exchange. Sophie wasn't able to travel all the way to Austin, but she was very interested in Prague – and hey, I was going to have an apartment there for a whole month anyway! Likewise, even though she visited my Prague apartment for only a weekend, she was willing to let me stay in her Paris apartment for longer, because she was going to be out of town for work anyway, and it was worth it to her to give me more time (when she would be gone regardless), in order to have her Prague weekend.

While I was in Europe that summer, I arranged two other exchanges – a simultaneous weekend exchange in Berlin, where I stayed in a very cool artist loft; and a two-bedroom apartment in Venice. The Venice exchange illustrated another situation that is not uncommon in the home exchange community. The apartment owner, Giorgio, was traveling for that entire month of August with his

Venice, Italy exchange apartment - August 2007

family, in northern Europe. He had no plans to ever visit Austin soon, but as he told me, the apartment would be empty anyway and he would be happy to have us stay there, even if he never used his exchange time with me. He felt better about having someone be in his apartment and watch over it than have it sit empty; also, as Giorgio put it, he strongly believed in the karma of such things. His hospitality to a visitor to Italy would be reciprocated by someone else, in another way, to him.

This is the type of person that you find in the home exchange community. Much like the homestay or hospitality community, it consists largely of open-minded frequent travelers who enjoy opening their homes and themselves to other people and cultures, and have a great attitude about it. Once Keith and I started traveling together, we also utilized housing swaps as our best method of traveling for free.

One of the things we are often asked about when we explain home exchanging to people is the possibility of crime, getting taken advantage of or ripped off. After our experiences of nearly two dozen exchanges, we can tell you that we now find it a rather silly question. First of all, you have a lot more chance of getting ripped off while walking down any city street – travel crime is much more likely to happen with stolen wallets or luggage. As far as personal property crime to your household, your home is far more likely to get cased and robbed by locals. Would someone really go to all the trouble to join a home exchange service, communicate and set up such an exchange with someone, and go to all that trouble to rob them? Really, there are far easier ways.

HomeExchange.com was the site used in the movie *The Holiday*, in which the entire plot centers around a home exchange between Cameron Diaz and Kate Winslet. An interesting movie if you're considering an exchange. Disclosure: Jude Law and Kate Winslet are usually not included.

Like most frequent and adventurous travelers, home exchangers are an open, friendly, curious lot who welcome the opportunity to travel to new and unexpected places themselves, as well as welcome visitors to their home. Many exchangers list second homes or vacation homes, meaning that because they do not live there full-time, they are much more flexible about when they exchange and non-simultaneous arrangements. Many exchangers are also retirees who spend a big part of their time traveling.

Our Panama City exchange – August 2013

Since that European summer of Shelley's first home exchanges over six years ago, we have gone on to do exchanges in Barcelona, Nicaragua, Mexico, Montreal, Vancouver, Seattle, Portland (three), Los Angeles, New York City (two), Washington D.C. and Hawaii. Just this summer, we took a two-month trip to South and Central America where we exchanged for a luxury, high-rise penthouse condo in Panama City (complete with daily maid service). *All completely for free.*

We've also done quick weekend exchanges closer to home, such as the Texas coast and San Antonio. Some of these exchanges have been simultaneous – the other party stayed in our place at the same time – and others have been non-simultaneous. It is really up to the parties to decide how and when they might want to do an exchange. Sometimes we also exchange cars, or take care of each other's pets. Again, all of this is up to discussion by the parties for any individual exchange.

We have completed our exchanges after a series of emails and phone calls with the other party, to feel comfortable about them and the potential exchange. However, you can go as far as you want with this; you could, if desired, require an application, background check, references and/or security deposit. Personally, we have never been asked for any of these things, nor asked for them, but those tools are at your disposal should you wish to use them when doing a home exchange.

Drew, musician and Hawaii exchange partner

Most exchangers leave an instruction sheet with household details, such as information about security systems, trash days, hot tub or pool instructions, television or internet network instructions, etc. They will also leave any information about prior agreed-upon tasks such as watering plants or feeding pets. Most exchangers also leave information about their area, including public transit, their favorite restaurants, local grocery stores or things to do.

As mentioned, the huge benefit to home exchanging is that you are paying nothing for your accommodations – one of the two biggest expenses in traveling, along with airfare. This enables you to travel more frequently, and for longer times. Once you've paid your airfare, that doesn't change whether you are staying somewhere for two nights or two weeks; and with a home exchange, that cost is the same – zero. It is only dependent on the amount of time you work out with your exchange partner, and many exchangers are very open to and interested in longer term exchanges.

We have not stayed in a hotel for ten years. Using home exchange is an amazing way in which to live like a local, feel like a local and all at no cost. We have had successful home exchanges in San Francisco, Santa Cruz, New Orleans, Chicago, Washington D.C, New York, Paris, Amsterdam. For us the best feature is the ability to have non simultaneous exchanges and building up credits for future usage with other exchangers. We specifically look for home exchangers who have "second homes" which means they are usually very flexible with dates and ability to exchange at short notice.

--Peta Kaplan and Ben Sandzer-Bell, climateadaptationnow.org and greenglobaltrek.blogspot.com

I found my first house swap on craigslist in 2007. I was in dire need of a 'break' from my normal routine but didn't have a lot of money to run away. I found a woman considering relocating from Kona, on the Big Island of Hawaii, to Austin to look for job. We agreed to swap for a month, cars included. I had her amazing ocean view from her apartment in Kona, she had my newly remodeled cool condo close to downtown Austin. We were both happy in our new places and ended up extending our stays for six months. It was an amazing experience living for FREE in Hawaii for six months. Would not have been able to have that extended 'break' without a house swap.

--Marnie Long, mdesignstudio.com

Although we initially started exchanging due to the money factor, we quickly found that it was only one of many major benefits. First of all, there are other cost savings involved. If you also exchange a car or use your exchange partner's car, you are saving a huge amount of money on car rental. There are also potentially big savings on food – because you are staying in a home with a kitchen, you can do a lot of eating in, saving big money on restaurant bills. Even if you're not interested in cooking at your exchange accommodations, at the very least you can buy breakfast, lunch or snack items at a local grocery store and save having to eat out for three meals a day. This is especially important for families.

The other big advantage for families is the space. While home exchanges can run the gamut from tiny studio apartments to huge six-bedroom houses, a family can very easily find a two or three bedroom home that will accommodate them – and which is much, much more comfortable than a hotel room or suite.

When completing your home exchange listing, be sure and include a photo of yourself along with your house photos. People really like putting a face with the home, and it makes the process much more personal!

Along with that, you are staying in a home in a residential neighborhood, as opposed to a hotel in a tourist district. This gives the absolutely huge benefit of really living like a local, and experiencing the place in this way instead of being in the midst of the tourist areas. This aspect has greatly improved our travel experiences, especially when our exchange partners share their neighborhood favorites. I (Shelley) have eaten an exquisite meal in Venice, known as one of the most expensive cities in the world, off a tiny lane where we were the only non-Italian patrons, for less than $20. Prices in restaurants and shops located on main tourist drags, almost anywhere in the world, are priced accordingly; once you get off those drags and into the local neighborhoods, you not only ditch the tourist up-charge, but also get a more authentic experience as well.

The last unexpected benefit we have found with home exchanging is the interesting people we have met. We've exchanged with film directors, musicians, artists, wine merchants, people who build sustainable housing and other fascinating people. It is really fun to meet people like this (even when it's sometimes only virtually), and we have gotten to know some intriguing people we would never have otherwise come

Our exchange in Granada, Nicaragua – Jan. 2012

across. For example, Peta Kaplan and Ben Sandzer-Bell, whose own home exchange testimonial was shared on the previous page, were our hosts on a 2012 trip to Nicaragua. We stayed at their bamboo casita down the street from the main home where they lived, and it was great getting to know them and getting their insider tips on the city of Granada. We went out to dinner with them one night to their favorite restaurant, and had a great time. More than a year and a half later, we are still in touch with Peta and Ben, who recently moved to Vietnam.

Clearly, we are huge fans of home exchanges. Your success rate depends in large part on where your home is located; obviously, the more in-demand its location, the more offers and acceptances of your offers you will receive. New York and Paris residents, clearly, will have a big advantage over someone in a small city without many tourist attractions. However, a lot of people use home exchanges for many different reasons besides vacationing in top destinations – they want to visit family or friends, or attend a certain conference or festival. You will find exchanges in virtually any and all destinations. It may or may not be right for you, but it's well worth looking into and considering. **You can read Shelley's article on the subject at Transitions Abroad (15).**

Home Exchange Resources:

- HomeExchange.com – In my opinion the biggest and best; I have arranged all but three of my exchanges through this site. Membership is $10/month (payable annually), but if you don't complete a home exchange your first year, they'll give you the second year for free.
- Digsville.com – Thousands of listings in 53 countries, though not nearly as many as HomeExchange. I have done two exchanges through this service. Membership is $45/year.
- ihen.com – A little more geared toward users outside the U.S., and they also list vacation rentals. $40/year.
- HomeForExchange.com – Europe-based network with over 13,000 listings. $65/year with an offer of second year free if you don't arrange an exchange in your first year.
- HomeLink.org – Over 13,000 members in 72 countries; $39-89/year.
- Knok.com – This is a brand new exchange site that we just learned about prior to publication of this updated book. It seems to have great potential; more than 30,000 homes in 159 countries as of this writing. Home insurance is included.
- Global Home Exchange – Membership levels for $10/month of $36/year.
- Craigslist.org – Exchanges can definitely be found through this site; I have done one this way. There is no cost associated, but beware that craigslist is infamous for scammers, so exercise caution.

"Without new experiences, something inside of us sleeps. The sleeper must awaken." ~Frank Herbert

HOUSE SITTING & CARETAKER SERVICES

This is another great option to consider that usually involves completely free stays. Similar to home exchanging in that you are staying in someone else's house, the difference is that they are not coming to your house. Many people who travel extensively, have second homes, take a temporary job or project, or otherwise have a need to be away from their homes for relatively long periods of time often search for house sitters to stay at their homes and take care of things, rather than letting them sit empty. People who look for  caretakers do so for reasons as varied as having things that need to be taken special care of, from pets to gardens; to owning a very nice, high-end home that they do not want to leave unsupervised; and many other reasons.

Most of the time people who search for caretakers, rather than doing a home exchange, is because they already have housing situated in the place they are going, and it may be a one-time situation for them (rather than home exchangers, who often exchange over and over again, like us). There are caretakers who make professional careers out of this, marketing their house sitting services all over the world and building a business out of referrals.

Unlike most home exchange situations, if you apply to be a house sitter or caretaker there will usually be an application process involved. You will most likely be asked to fill out information about yourself and provide references. Sometimes, such a position will even pay a small stipend or additional wage besides the included housing; this usually depends on what type of work, if any, the caretaker is being asked to do around the property.

One area that is typically dependent on each situation and possibly up for negotiation is the issue of bills. With a home exchange, most of the time each homeowner continues to pay the bills on their own properties. But with house sitting, depending on the length of the arrangement and the agreement between the parties, a caretaker may be responsible for some of their own bills, including utilities, internet, television or telephone. Also, sometimes insurance, a bond, or a deposit may be required by the homeowner as security.

Caretaking and home exchanging are both excellent options to consider for long-term travel. A person could easily spend six months, a year, or even several years moving around the world and staying in these types of situations for weeks or months at a time.

One of the great things about house sitting, though, is that there are a wide range of opportunities

Check out the awesome story on Huffington Post (16), of how one couple traveled the world without paying a penny for accommodations — all done through housesitting!

available from long-term caretaker situations to a weekend house sit. The keys to landing these opportunities include:

- A solid profile on the sites you use, with a lot of information about yourself and your experience (both as a caretaker, house sitter, maintaining your own home and with pets).

- Opening email to your potential jobs where you reference their specific needs and details, and how you can benefit them.

- Provide references, whether for previous sitting or just those who can speak highly to your reliability and responsibility. Landlords and work colleagues make good references.

- Be prepared by asking plenty of questions before starting a house sit or caretaking gig, and make sure you have all necessary instructions, your questions are answered, and any emergency contact information.

Caretaking/House Sitting Resources:

- Caretaker.org – The only publication in the world dedicated to the property caretaking field. Published since 1983, this is a bimonthly newsletter that lists hundreds of caretaking opportunities around the world in each issue, and can be accessed both online and via the printed subscription. $29.95-43.95 per year; highly recommended.
- HouseCarers.com – Matches homeowners with sitters; free for homeowners, membership fee of $50/year to advertise your house sitting availability or services and contact homeowners to apply for their openings. Can do a non-paid listing to start (must pay to contact others).
- HouseSittersAmerica.com – For U.S. listings, this website connects homeowners and house sitters in all 50 states. Free for property owners; $30/year for house sitters.
- MindMyHouse.com – A global matching service for owners and caretakers; sitters can search listings for free, or advertise their services for $20/year.
- SabbaticalHomes.com – The academic community's resource for home exchanges and house sitters worldwide. This site lists all sorts of opportunities, including paid monthly rentals and no-cost caretaking situations.
- TrustedHousesitters.com – Helping pet and home owners find trusted sitters.

HOMESTAYS/COUCH SURFING/HOSPITALITY EXCHANGE

A typical homestay involves staying as a paying guest in someone's home, at a nightly or weekly rate that is typically very inexpensive (often $10-15 per night). While it may sound similar to a bed & breakfast, homestays are much more informal. You are usually the only guest, and the place is the host's actual everyday home, as opposed to a property that is run primarily as an inn with several rooms (even if the proprietors live on-site, as is the case with many B&Bs).

Homestays used to be most common among students and young travelers; the image of a foreign exchange student comes to mind. These days, however, many people of all ages take advantage of homestays, including couples, families and friends traveling together. The benefits are numerous, particularly if you enjoy making new friends and interacting with others. First of all, the cost is usually nominal. Second, it is a true cultural immersion – you are living with a host or family, seeing the place through their eyes and often meeting their friends, eating meals with them, and discovering the area with them or on their advised itinerary. This allows you to really discover a place off the beaten path. If you are trying to learn a language, this option can't be beat for total immersion; in fact, many homestay agencies exist solely to match guests in such placements for immersion language lessons. You might leave a homestay with some new language skills, knowing how to cook regional specialties like a local, and lifelong friends that you leave more as a member of the family than paying guest.

If you are a much more private person who prefers to be left to your own devices, a homestay might not be the best choice for you; however, as with most travel options, homestays can offer a wide range between very sociable hosting and the simple provision of room and board, after which you are left alone. Also, because you are staying in someone's home, you When arriving as a guest at a homestay, it's a nice gesture to bring your hosts a small, inexpensive token gift from where you live.

may need to abide by certain rules and need to exercise special respect for your host's wishes (for example: curfews, bathroom privileges or alcohol consumption). By looking through various listings and a bit of communication with a potential host, you can easily determine if the situation meets your expectations and travel style.

Again, homestays are very inexpensive – and there are even hospitality exchange clubs that you can join, offering membership benefits such as stays for no charge at all. This is also known as "couch surfing" – people who offer traveling visitors a couch or bed to sleep on at no charge, often enjoying the opportunity to show the visitor around their town and make a new friend. With couch surfing, often your accommodations are more limited – perhaps you get your own bedroom, perhaps you do literally sleep on the couch. Likewise, many couch surfers operate like a hospitality exchange: at your discretion you offer to let others within a pool of people stay with you at another date, as pay back for you getting to stay with someone else within that same pool. You host a traveler, you stay as a traveler. Read Robert Firpo-Cappiello's "Confessions of a Couchsurfer" (17) at *Budget Travel* for an inside look.

We know many people who swear by couch surfing, and utilize it extensively when traveling. Our friend Jefre Outlaw, who was the keynote speaker at a MeetPlanGo.com event we hosted last year, has been to more than 100 countries and couch surfs all the time. In fact, Jefre reports that he does about 50% hostel stays and 50% couch surfing on his travels. This is a sure-fire way to not only get completely free accommodations, but to meet locals who can tell you about, and often show you around, their town.

The largest and most recognized homestay organization is international HomestayAgency.com. Here you can view and contact potential hosts, as well as sign up to provide a homestay if you are interested in meeting and hosting travelers from around the world yourself. WorldHomestay.com offers a great set of tips for homestay guests. There are also many other excellent websites for homestays on the next page.

After couch surfing in 75 countries I am the most experienced CS traveler I have met so far. My advice here is for people to build complete profiles and use the site often for not just hosting or being hosted but meeting people for lunch, dinner, drinks, coffee, etc. It is a social networking community for travel addicts.

--Jefre Outlaw (Find him at Facebook.com/jefre.outlaw)

Homestay Resources:

- cci-exchange.com: Independent short-term homestays
- CouchSurfing.com: By far the most popular; worldwide network of hosts offering their couches (or a room) for visiting travelers
- GlobalFreeloaders.com: Free homestay accommodations around the world
- GoHomestay.com: Homestay listings around the world
- HospitalityClub.org: Free membership club with members around the world
- Hospex.net: Members offer homestays around the world (paid membership)
- HomestayAgency.com: Homestay listings around the world
- lghei.org: Homestays for gay and lesbian travelers (paid membership)
- servas.org: The oldest homestay organization with members around the world (paid membership)
- TransitionsAbroad.com: Links, articles and other homestay resources
- Tripping.com: Global travel hosting community for not only homestays, but also connect for rideshares, meeting locals for coffee or meals, and travel tips!
- womenwelcomewomen.org.uk: Homestays for women (paid membership)
- WorldHomestay.com: Homestays around the world (paid membership)

CAMPING

Many people who desire and plan to travel internationally for longer or more frequent periods of time, are people who have already traveled pretty cheaply around home. The same principles apply when trying to travel on a budget – think about the local trips you have taken that were super-cheap, or the types of travel you may have done back in college.

Camping is one of the least expensive ways that people go out and spend a weekend away when they are at home; but you can also camp many places around the world, and it's a viable option especially if you really like the outdoors. And in many other

Canvas Holidays, a UK based camping website, offers some great free resources such as FamilyExtra (free activity programs for kids and their parents, 18) and a Free Guide to Camping (19).

countries, public transportation is much better, meaning that you might not even have to rent a car to get to camping spots.

Campgrounds for both vehicles and tents (and that offer tented accommodations) are plentiful throughout Europe, Australia, New Zealand, South Africa, Canada and the United States. And of course, besides official paying campgrounds there is also the option of "wild" or "stealth" camping – just camping independently, on the go, for free. Bicyclists and backpackers often utilize wild camping, although of course there is much more to take into consideration: safety, hassle from local police, and wild animals.

Our friends over at Travelling Two offer some tips for wild camping (20). And head over to BootsnAll Travel for a list of The 8 Best Places to Camp Around the World (21).

Some resources for finding camp accommodations include:

- Landal.com (Europe)
- CanvasHolidays.co.uk (Europe)
- CampingEurope.com (Europe)
- FreeCampgrounds.com (USA)
- GoCampingAmerica.com (USA)
- KOA.com (USA)
- FreeCampsites.net
- WorldCampsites.com
- CampingCardInternational.com
- LovetheOutdoors.com
- OzBackpackerTours.com.au (camping and hostel info around Australia)

When we travel we camp a lot. This saves us a TON of money. I've heard many horror stories (sore backs, leaks, coldness, ect) from others that have tried camping and they have indeed sounded horrible. BUT - if you get proper gear I find camping to be preferable in many instances. I don't have worry about when the last time a blanket on a bed was washed, no noisy midnight doors slamming in paper thin hallways, listening directly to the sounds of waves crashing, rivers running and what have you. Camping draws a certain amount of welcome attention. In a lot of instances the majority of travelers don't camp, so when you're in the minority that do, locals are interested and conversations start that wouldn't have other wise. This has lead to invitations and contacts with locals. The key most important thing about camping is to find the gear that you love and works for you. When I have to replace gear I often buy the same exact item again because I know it will serve me well. Camping has allowed us to literally travel for months on end where as paying for hotels, hostels or having to make a very specific itinerary with couch surfing would have prohibited us a lot more from exploring.

--Tiffany Soukup & Christopher Brader, Vagabondway.net

HOSTELS

Hostels are a fantastic and often overlooked potential choice for people traveling on more limited budgets. For those who might cringe at the thought of staying at a hostel, please realize that the definition of a hostel has been broadened dramatically in recent years. It used to solely mean dormitory room accommodations with shared bathrooms, restrictive rules, and availability limited to people under 25 years of age. It may have been a great choice for young backpackers but maybe not for others. Now most hostels are open to people of all ages, including seniors and those with children, and the actual accommodations range from stereotypical dorm rooms with basic amenities to private single and double rooms with their own bathrooms in much smaller, more unique environments.

Most hostels provide the absolute cheapest option for paid accommodations. Very decent hostels can be had around the world for less than $20 per night if you are in a shared dorm room; and many of these offer privacy curtains, reading lights and electrical outlets at each bed, so you can have a certain degree of privacy. Most of the time the toilets and showers, while shared, are private – so when you have use of a bathroom, you are not using the facilities with others. Most hostels today welcome families, children and seniors, and private rooms and bathrooms are not uncommon – more expensive than the shared dorm rooms, but still way cheaper than a hotel.. Many, in fact, are actually budget hotels that have rebranded themselves to broaden their market appeal.

Another benefit of a hostel, especially if you are a very social person, is the sense of community and traveling camaraderie that they share. They have common spaces where the guests tend to congregate for eating, watching movies, playing games, getting on the internet and swapping travel tales.

Breakfast is usually included, and very frequently regular group dinners are as well (sometimes an extra fee). Kitchens are often available for guests to use, store food and cook, and a great many hostel travelers stay at them not only for the cheap rates, but the ability to meet other travelers from all over the world, and sometimes make lifelong friends. Some of the best insider tips on the local area and free or under-the-radar things to do are to be had by talking with fellow travelers. Most hostels also put together outings and tours to local attractions, as well as parties and other social events at the hostel.

The best bet for a free stay at a hostel is to work for it. This isn't usually an option for short-term travel, but if you can stay and work for at least a week or two, many hostels offer work exchanges. A few resources to check out include HostelWorld.com, HIhostels.com and HostelBookers.com, global networks of thousands of hostels around the world, many of which offer work/trade opportunities. Of course you can also check with non-HI affiliated hostels as well. And at HostelManagement.com, there is a forum for hostel jobs around the world. More details about what to expect when exchanging work for travel are found in the next chapter.

Lastly, there are some very, very hip and cool hostels. Some can be found in historical buildings with amazing architecture; others revolve around themes such as art or music. Here is a list of some stand-out hostels around the world:

- **Slovenia: <u>Hostel Celica</u>.** This used to be a military prison, and rooms still have the original cell bars on windows and doors. It's a haven for creative types, with an art gallery, concerts and poetry readings. Voted hippest hostel by *Lonely Planet*.

- **Sweden: <u>Jumbo Stay</u>.** Located at the Stockholm Airport, this upscale hostel created out of a Boeing 747 is maybe one of the most unique accommodations in the world. And only a 10-minute walk from the ticket counters!

- **China: <u>Zhangzhou Wei Qun Lou Inn</u>.** This amazing building is listed on the World Heritage Sites, and is a miracle in the history of world architecture. It is a symbol of the wisdom and diligence of the Hakka people who built it.

- **Mongolia: <u>Anak Ranch</u>.** To experience an ancient, little known way of life, stay in these traditional nomad homes called gers, where you can also learn how to work a ranch, Mongolian-style.

- **Australia: <u>Radecka Underground Mine Hostel</u>**. This is actually an old working opal mine from the 1960s, no joke, that has been turned into an underground hostel in the Australian Outback. Really.

- **California: <u>Point Montara Lighthouse Hostel</u>**. 25 miles south of San Francisco, this historic lighthouse is perched on a bluff overlooking the Pacific Ocean, and offers an idyllic retreat for exploring outdoor recreation in the area.

MONASTERIES & CONVENTS

Believe it or not, monasteries and convents can be great options for low-cost accommodations, particularly throughout Europe. Often they operate on a donation basis, allowing you to pay what you wish or what you can afford. Many monasteries offer guest rooms, and although the

lodging is usually simple and basic (often even spartan), they are clean, safe and give a glimpse into a local way of life that few get to see. Many such rooms offer private or semi-private baths. Just like B&B inns, however, monasteries can range from quite austere to incredibly luxurious.

These types of accommodations have long been popular with European travelers, and are also great options for women traveling alone (22). The rates are generally along the lines of a hostel, and some post a suggested donation as opposed to a fixed rate. They are very often housed in incredibly historic, beautiful buildings, and run by "real" monks and nuns who are members of the community and go about their daily business while you are their guest. There is no religious requirement, affiliation or expectation of guests. You will not be asked about your religion but are usually welcome to attend community services if you wish. Some convents or monasteries do have curfew times at night, so please check all policies.

Monastery/Convent Lodging Resources:

- MonasteryStays.com is a great website for finding such lodging in Italy (one of the best places for this), and it also provides a wealth of general information, articles and videos about what it's like to stay in a monastery.
- Travel author Eileen Barish has a great blog called the Monastery Lodging Blog at eileenbarish.net.
- You might not think it, but there are monastery inns in the United States as well – even in Oklahoma! (23)
- From Matador Network, this is a great article highlighting 15 Monastery Stays around the world (24).
- This USA Today Travel Tips article gives some nice tips about staying in monasteries (25).

FARMS & AGRICULTURAL STAYS

Here's another lodging option you may not have thought about, that also provides a very unique stay with a glimpse into a local, traditional way of life, at costs that are usually very low. Many farms and agricultural collectives around the world offer accommodations, to such an extent that this type of travel has a name for it: agrotourism. You will also hear it referred to as farmstays, and they can be found on both working and non-working farms.

One of the beauties of such a stay is the wide variety of types of farms and activities you have the opportunity to encounter across the world. For example, farms in Vermont offer dairy milking and apple picking. On the farms of Skarsmoen in Scandinavia, you could take part in moose safaris and learn how to make cheese. In Germany you can stay in a barn, literally sleeping on a haystack, and take multi-day bicycling trips around the region. And in Italy, you could stay at a vineyard and assist in grape stomping and wine making if you choose – and of course, tasting!

Agrisport.com is a website that lists farmstays around the world; as does AgritourismWorld.com, a site which lets you search by either geographical location, or category of the type of experience you are interested in.

As with B&Bs and hostels, the best way to get free accommodations on a farmstay is by working. Fortunately, there is an excellent and extensive website to help you find such an agricultural work exchange. WWOOF.org (World Wide Opportunities on Organic Farms) is dedicated to the international movement for sustainable living, and lists thousands of exchange opportunities where you can volunteer on an organic farm in return for lodging and, very often, meals.

"Once in a while it really hits people that they don't have to experience the world in the way they have been told to." ~Alan Keightley

VACATION RENTALS

House, condo, apartment and villa rentals can be excellent alternatives to staying in a hotel for several reasons. They are often much less expensive than paying for a hotel or resort, especially if you will be in Western Europe where accommodation prices tend to be higher and/or if you have a large group or family where you will need more than one room. And additional savings can be had from using the kitchen instead of eating at restaurants for every meal, possibly free parking, no tipping, etc. Also, some people prefer the atmosphere and feel of being in a home-like atmosphere as opposed to being in a more commercialized establishment. Likewise by going this route you have a better chance of meeting more locals and doing more of the things that locals do. And with the difficult economy and the recent pop of the real estate bubble there are more and more properties being rented out, some of which are in some very beautiful locations and offered at better rates than they once were.

Like small inns and B&Bs, renting a vacation home or condo can range across a very wide spectrum, from simple and economical properties to the wildly lavish. Also, the best ways to stay in these types of properties for free or very cheaply are also the work exchange and barter options mentioned in the next chapter. Some of the top sites for finding homes and other vacation properties to rent are:

- Airbnb.com
- VRBO.com
- HouseTrip.com (primarily Europe, but expanding)
- HomeAway.com
- FlipKey.com
- Roomerama.com

Of these sites, by far our favorite (and the only one we've used a lot) is Airbnb. In fact, in our opinion doing vacation rentals can be the second best and easiest way, after home exchange, to get accommodations completely for free. What we mean by this is, with home exchange of course a successful exchange depends on finding someone who wants to come to your destination and stay in your home; but with vacation rentals, that doesn't matter. If you can rent your place out

You can stay at the world's weirdest building, in London! https://www.airbnb.com/rooms/571023

during the time you will be gone, then you can use that money to rent your own place in your destination.

I (Shelley) have done this many times. Particularly, it is successful when I travel during periods of time when tourism is at a peak high in my hometown. Here in Austin, festivals and events such as SXSW, the ACL Music Festival and Formula 1 races draw thousands from all over the world, and short-term vacation rentals are at a premium. Many, many times (in fact, during virtually all of these events) I have listed my place on Airbnb and booked a guest for a nice little chunk of money - $100 to $300 per night depending on the dates. I then use the money I earn as a host, to fund my own travel somewhere else. Voila – a free trip! And, there are some *really* cool places to stay on Airbnb (26) – how about an Airstream trailer, a palace, lighthouse, windmill, teepee, gypsy wagon, bedoin tent, covered bridge, or even a historic beer barrel?

We are currently travelling the world for better than free! Instead of the home exchange option, we have rented out our apartment in Australia. This means we can travel forever as long as we spend less than the rent. In Southeast Asia, we make a profit. We are nearing the end of our 2nd year of continuous travel and have decided to do a Year 3. We stay in budget hotels, with family, friends, Airbnb, Couch Surfing, find good deals, etc. We have been to Wimbledon, Tour de France, Running of the Bulls, and the Olympics. We also threw in the 50th Anniversary Beatles Festival, the Edinburgh Fringe Festival, heaps of time in Europe, a European cruise, Egypt and a Nile cruise, the Middle East, a cruise from Dubai to Singapore, Bali, and more. We have 'blown our budget' but that doesn't matter because overall, due to the rent coming in, we still spend less than if we were bored and retired at home."

--Jon and Jenny Stark, TeachorBeach.com

BED & BREAKFAST INNS

Long the preferred method of accommodation in Europe before becoming a popular option in the US for quaint lodging with personal attention, B&Bs offer a fairly wide variety of accommodations compared to the narrow definition some people may have. Although they all typically include breakfast and offer a relatively small number of rooms compared to a hotel, not all fit the stereotype of having a folksy, homey, grandma's house feel. Some are more contemporary. Some are more historically themed due to their particular location. Some are on working farms or vineyards. Some are more rustic while others are luxurious. The point is that the experiences available are very diverse, and with the internet you should be able to easily find out what the individual properties offer.

It should be noted that while in general B&Bs tend to be less expensive than hotels – particularly in Europe – this is not always the case. B&Bs have a wide variety of styles, service and price ranges, and can provide budget travel, or an option as expensive as the hotels. In Europe, you may hear a B&B referred to as a *pensione*, the more typical term for what is essentially the same thing. A pensione is a family-run guest or boarding house, typically offering breakfast and often other meals, and is comparable to the American bed & breakfast inn.

The best ways to get free or very inexpensive accommodations at small inns and B&Bs are to find small, simple, individually-run places outside large cities; and to use some of the options explored in the next chapter for work exchange, bartering or volunteering in return for accommodations. Some good websites are:

- BedandBreakfast.com
- JustBedandBreakfast.net
- BBGetaways.com (U.S. only)
- 1BBweb.com
- BBTravel.com

HOTELS

Hotels and resorts are often the first types of lodging that people think of when they need a place to stay, and for many situations they are the perfect solution. They range from the very basic to the most opulent, and pricing can be all over the map, often times even for the exact same room. Fortunately since they are the most prevalent form of lodging they also have some of the most useful websites available to help you make your choices. On the down side, choosing hotel accommodations is the most expensive option, and the least flexible in terms of being able to secure free or next-to-free lodging.

We often stay at hotels for free, but that is because Shelley is a professional travel journalist and often writes published reviews of hotels, and Keith does the photography. Free hotel stays are also often available for people in the travel industry; for example, travel agents who are given "fam" trips and comped rooms. Granted, this is not something that most people have available to them. However, there are still a few potential ways that the typical, non-travel-industry person can stay in hotels for free or very cheap:

- **Join a Hotel Loyalty Reward Program.** Just like airline miles programs, many hotel chains and groups offer the same type of customer loyalty programs where you can earn points for future free stays. Check with any hotel companies at which you've already stayed frequently, to begin with; you may have already accumulated points. The best bets are with the largest programs that offer the biggest number of hotel selections. Some of the major ones are Club Carlson, Choice Privileges, Starwood, Hilton Honors, Marriott Rewards, Hyatt Gold Passport and Priority Club. One of the largest is TripRewards.com, with over 6,000 mostly budget participating hotels throughout the world. For the independent traveler doing U.S. travel, StashRewards.com gets our vote. Rather than chain brands, Stash focuses on one-of-a-kind, unique hotels in the U.S. with a points system that earns free nights. There's also a great "cheat sheet" of hotel rewards programs at NerdWallet.com.

- **Use Frequent Flyer Miles.** Don't forget that your airline miles don't have to be used only for flights; you can also often use frequent flyer points to book hotel stays and other travel. Here is an excellent step-by-step article from Ehow.com on using airline miles to book hotels (27).

- **Become a Mystery Shopper.** There are numerous companies that provide blind shopping services for all kinds of businesses, from hotels to restaurants, retail stores and movie theaters. The professional shopper visits the business just as any other customer would, and reports back on his or her experience. You probably would not be comped or reimbursed for more than one night's stay as a shopper, but it's worth checking into. See the "Become a Mystery Shopper" section in the next chapter for more details and resources.

"There are no foreign lands. It is the traveler only who is foreign." ~Robert Louis Stevenson

THE GOOD OLD FRIEND NETWORK

Last but not least, don't overlook the oldest networking tool in the world – the friend network. If you have plans to travel anywhere, but particularly any sort of extended travel, send out an announcement to everyone you know about your plans. You don't have to actually ask for free accommodations, but you can definitely let people know that you are looking for places to stay and would appreciate referrals or introductions to anyone in the areas you are traveling to, who might be able to make a recommendation. You might be surprised by how many people invite you to stay with them, or knows someone whose house is empty and could use a house sitter, or at the very least knows of a great, inexpensive B&B or hostel to tell you about.

Besides accommodations, this is a great way to get introductions to people in the places you are traveling to, which makes your journey all the more fun – particularly if you are going to foreign or adventurous destinations that you have never been to before. Through the whole "friend-of-a-friend, pass-it-on" networking tool, you might meet up with a local in Stockholm for coffee, or have a friend's cousin in Beijing show you around for a day. And this is so easy to do in today's technology age – you can send out an email, post it on social networking sites such as Facebook and twitter, or even start your own travel blog.

Brainstorm Session – Creative Lodging Ideas:

_____

_____

_____

_____

_____

_____

_____

_____

_____

_____

Packing Checklist from Doug Dyment's Excellent "One Bag" Website:

dressy jacket

2-4 shirts/blouses/tops

2 pairs trousers/skirts (shorts?)

3+ pairs socks

3+ pairs undergarments

long (lightweight) underwear

swimsuit

dark (cardigan) sweater

rainwear (umbrella?)

parka, coat, or equivalent

long T-shirt or sarong [cover-up]

necktie, scarf, hairband, bandanna

gloves / mittens

sun hat / knitted cap, hat clip

1 pair dressy shoes (laces?)

1 pair walking shoes/boots (laces?)

flip-flops or sandals

belt

travel pack or shoulder bag (& luggage cart?)

daypack (fanny pack? purse?)

lightweight duffel/laundry bag

luggage lock(s) (cable?)

alarm clock/watch (batteries?)

flashlight, headstrap, extra batteries (bulbs?)

multipurpose tool, scissors

spoon (fork? chopsticks? spork?), (coffee tin lid) plate or bowl

compass

whistle

door stop [for security]

inflatable travel pillow

hostel sheet bag (sleeping bag? bivouac sack? blanket? tent?)

safety pins, rubber bands, cord

sewing kit, including large needle to accommodate dental floss

(Ziploc®) plastic bags, garbage bags

duct/gaffer's tape (packing tape?)

toothbrush, cap, tooth cleaner, floss

razor, blades, shaving oil/cream

comb and/or hairbrush

shampoo, bar soap & container

deodorant

nail clippers

[unbreakable] mirror

viscose towel (washcloth?)

universal (flat) sink stopper

detergent, spot remover

(surgical latex braid) clothesline (carabiner?)

inflatable hangers [to dry clothes]

toilet paper, water squirt bottle, antibacterial wipes

(chemical or mechanical) water purifier

analgesic of choice

diarrhea treatment of choice

infection treatment of choice

malaria tablets

insect repellent, mosquito net

sunscreen, lip balm

tweezers

bandages, moleskin (other first aid?)

menstrual, contraceptive, and/or prophylactic supplies

vitamins, necessary medications

(collapsible) plastic water bottle & cup

dark glasses, retainer, case

lens cleaning cloth/supplies, copy of prescription (spare glasses?)

earplugs (eye mask?) [to ease sleep]

pen(s), small notebook, glue stick [for notes, addresses, diary, ...]

personal address book (stamps?)

maps, guidebooks, phrase books, Post-it® notes, restaurant lists, membership cards, business/calling cards, telephone access numbers

reading material

large envelopes [to mail things home]

passport, visas, extra passport photos, vaccination certificates

copies of important documents

(international?) driver's license, health insurance information

travel tickets

charge & ATM cards, cash (traveller's cheques?)

2 personal cheques

security pouch [worn under clothes]

Specialty Items:

camera (lenses? flash? tripod? extra cards & batteries? charger? download adapter?)

cellular telephone (charger?)

laptop computer (flash drive? power cord/adapters? network cable(s)?)

(solar) calculator

gifts

"Arriving at each new city, the traveler finds again a past of his that he did not know he had: the foreignness of what you no longer are or no longer possess lies in wait for you in foreign, unpossessed places." ~Italo Calvino

CREATIVE WAYS TO TRAVEL

WORKING AS YOU TRAVEL

One of the biggest potential obstacles to long-term travel is being able to sustain yourself financially while no longer having a 'regular' job. We hear this from people who work for someone else as well as from people who work for themselves.

Many accommodations will offer the opportunity to work in exchange for your lodging — just as long as you put a little sweat into it. In fact, working to earn your stay isn't just about saving money. Doing so is one of the best ways to integrate more deeply into a culture and experience all it has to offer firsthand. No one will treat you like a tourist when they've watched you move bales of hay around all day!

"Work for stay" opportunities are typically found in smaller hotels, bed & breakfasts, and hostels; not so much in larger hotels or chains, especially for short-term work. Most places will want a commitment for at least a couple of weeks or longer – this is an option that works best when you want to travel and stay somewhere for a while, without having to pay anything. For obvious reasons, most inns or other lodging aren't interested in this type of arrangement for just a few days; the effort put forth to set it up and train you isn't worth it to them. But if you are interested in staying in a place for a few weeks to a few months, this could be a great option for free accommodations. Typical jobs would be cleaning, front desk reception, kitchen/cooking or maintenance/handyman work. Keep in mind that we are talking about short-term, informal work trades; working full-time, for very long-term, or at a large establishment for an official paycheck would likely require a work permit and more formal employment procedures.

One specific type of working abroad that is very popular, and plentiful, is teaching. Most of these programs involve teaching English in countries all over the world, to both children and adults. This is one of the most common ways that thousands of people each year do working travel; generally, your travel expenses and accommodations are paid for, and teachers also

Photo courtesy of WorldTeach.org

receive a small stipend for monthly living expenses. You must generally be a college graduate and certified with a TEFL certification (Teaching English as a Foreign Language), though this is not always required. TEFL certification certainly helps you get a job, and better pay, however.

Keith lived in Japan for 5 months after college, where he taught English. His tips? Unless you already have connections in the country where you want to teach, it is probably best to line up a job before you arrive. A great website for learning about teaching overseas is eslcafe.com. Keep in mind that different countries have various high seasons for hiring. To increase your chances of landing a job, make sure you apply at the right time.

Another great resource is Helpx.net, an online listing service that matches working travelers with lodging, homestays, agricultural farms, B&Bs and even sailboats who need help in exchange for free lodging. WorkAway.info is another good resource, offering fair work trade between individuals and inns, farms, resorts and other individuals offering homestays. Or check out FrontierClub.com, a 40-year-old club that has been helping its members work their way around the world for decades.

Frontier Club is run by people who live this work/travel lifestyle themselves.

Other ideas for potential jobs to do as you travel include:

Bartender
Server
Delivery Person
Au pair
Travel Nurse
Farm/Ranch Worker
Camp Worker
International Aid or
Development
Dive Instructor
Ski Instructor or Resort Staff
Tour Guide
Cruise Ship Staff
Digital Nomad – working at
any sort of job you can do

> Check out the article on our blog: The Best Jobs that can Pay for your Travel (28). Other great resources for creatively funding travel include the BootsnAll Funding Your Travel Habit message boards (29); Wand'rly with How to Make a Living on the Road (30); and an article by our travel writer colleague Myscha Theriault on How to Make Money While Traveling (31) for more ideas.

remotely, such as software programming, marketing/PR, editing/writing, consulting, etc.

USA Today ran a great article about How to Travel for Free on a Sailboat, (32), and CNN likewise published How to Sail Around the World for Free (33) — from crew members and tutoring children to working on a research ship or cooking, there are many ways to sail your way around the world.

If you're really interested in working your way around the world, you probably want to follow Tucker of "AroundtheWorldin80Jobs.com." This guy set out abroad six years ago, looking to find a way of working and living internationally full-time. He's done everything from street tour and timeshare sales to farming, fishing and being a reality TV production assistant. He even worked as a tequila harvester in Mexico! His blog is pretty good at giving the true ins and outs of different kinds of work, and he's honest about whether he made any money and what jobs were complete failures (ex: Cuban Tobacco Farmer).

Finally, our friend and fellow travel blogger Nora Dunn, aka The Professional Hobo, has an ongoing series of Financial Travel Tips (34), sharing everything from tips on cheap accommodations, saving on transportation and going local to location independent businesses, travel insurance and the best travel credit cards. You can also get her free guide on How to Travel Fulltime in a Financially Sustainable Way at the same page!

Speaking of "digital nomads," there's another option when thinking about working your way around the world, rather than getting jobs and working for other people — and that is, to become an entrepreneur and set up your own location-independent business. There really are so many ways to generate income while not living at a fixed address, especially now given how wired the world is with the Internet. You can utilize tools such as Skype, Google Voice and Hangouts and other messaging/videoconferencing apps available today to stay connected and do business with people no matter where they — or you — are on the planet.

Some people take the skills they already have and become consultants; others set up a new business, sometimes alongside their newfound travel lifestyle, such as selling their travel photography or sourcing local jewelry and handicrafts for resale. Basically, we both have done this, building our own self-employed businesses that we can conduct on the road or from wherever we have an Internet connection.

The ability to travel is core to our lifestyle. Therefore for the past ten years we have sought to develop careers which are conducive to travel, blurring the line between work and travel. This is a variant on the theme of "making money on the road." We started a bamboo housing business in Nicaragua, Central America with the expectation that our work and travel model would lead us to travel to bamboo destinations around the world. Indeed, as a result we have travelled to Ecuador, Panama, Colombia, Haiti, Dominican Republic, France and Holland and connected with others in our field of work in those countries. In many cases our "cost of travel" was greatly reduced as a result of hospitality offered to us by others in our line of work and the ability to write off travel expenses as work related.
--Peta Kaplan and Ben Sandzer-Bell, climateadaptationnow.org & greenglobaltrek.blogspot.com

There are several resources that we have found incredibly helpful for people looking to start a new business. Chris Guillebeau is a successful serial micro-entrepreneur and the inspirational blogger on his awesome website, The Art Of Non-Conformity. For years now he has been providing unconventional strategies for life, work and travel. He's a huge traveler himself having already visited all 193 countries in the world! And he recently came out with a new book titled *The $100 Startup* that shows you how to lead a life of adventure, meaning and purpose while still earning a good living.

Read our interview with Chris Guillebeau on our blog (35).

In a nutshell, *The $100 Startup* lays out concrete ideas and instructions on how to create and market a unique offering of goods and/or services that provide real value to customers who are willing to pay you for them. And throughout all these insights Chris weaves in 50 interesting, real-life, case studies on how people like you and me were able to find their niche and restructure their lives to be able to do the things they want to do.

Another excellent source for crafting both a business and a life to be self-supporting (and location independent if you choose), is the continually helpful *4 Hour Workweek* by Timothy Ferriss. Forget the old concept of retirement and the rest of the deferred-life plan–there is no need to wait and every reason not to, especially in unpredictable economic times. Whether your dream is escaping the rat race, experiencing high-end world travel, earning a monthly five-figure income with zero management, or just living more and working less, The 4-Hour Workweek is the blueprint. We have both used this book in figuring out our life and work strategies.

"Adventure is a path. Real adventure – self-determined, self-motivated, often risky – forces you to have firsthand encounters with the world. The world the way it is, not the way you imagine it. This will change you. Nothing will ever again be black-and-white." ~Mark Jenkins

 More Work Abroad Resources:

- BackdoorJobs.com is a fantastic resource with a large database of work opportunities in the U.S. and all over the world. How about working on a yacht or as a dive instructor? Maybe you'd like to lead adventure trips in hiking, biking or kayaking – or lead teens in such wilderness adventures. Or perhaps you've considered teaching abroad or working on a cruise ship. Backdoor Jobs has them all, in a very complete and user-friendly website.
- HostelManagement.com is a forum for hostel jobs around the world.
- TransitionsAbroad.com has a great section on Working Abroad, from informative articles, resources, and listings for jobs all over the world.
- CIEE.org is a well-known and respected international exchange program for students, providing information and exchange matches for working, studying and traveling abroad.
- BUNAC.org bills itself as Working Adventures Worldwide. They offer a range of exciting work and volunteer abroad programs around the world.
- CCUSA.com is an international work adventure specialist, providing opportunities for summer camp jobs as well as other work/travel and volunteer experiences in more than 60 countries.
- Helpx.net is an online listing of host farms, homestays, ranches, lodges, B&Bs, hostels and even boats who invite people to work in exchange for accommodation and food.
- WorkAway.info is a great site for travel, work exchange and language learning. They promote fair exchange between budget travelers who want to exchange work for travel.
- Matador Network has a great article about how to travel for free as a work camper (36) – a great outdoor lifestyle perfect for those who enjoy camping and want to fund their sustained travel. National parks, park management companies and private campgrounds are all listed as great sources for this type of work/travel.

- WorldTeach.org features long-term teaching opportunities abroad, both for younger people and also for mid-career and retired teachers.
- Workamper.com is a great resource for those wanting to travel and work at camps.
- JobsAbroad.com has a lot of work abroad opportunities listed around the world; listings are heavy on English teaching and nanny positions.
-
- InterExchange.org is another website that likely lists a lot of the same companies and opportunities, but it's probably worth checking both.
- TESOL-UA.org is the certification for TEFL (Teaching English as a Foreign Language), and is the first step to teaching abroad. Site has certification info as well as teaching opportunities.
- ESLcafe.com is a great resource for learning all about teaching English abroad.
- Workingyourwayaroundtheworld.com blog is written by Thursday Bram, author of a book by the same name. In the blog she shares tips and her experiences for how to work around the world, from far-flung jobs to telecommuting or starting your own business.
- AllianceAbroad.com is the leader in international recruitment to the United States (for those living in other countries and looking to work here), helping participants find work or training and secure their J-1 visas.
- WWOOFusa.org (Worldwide Organization of Organic Farmers) pairs workers with farms worldwide who are looking for workers, in exchange for free accommodations.
- FindaCrew.net is a site that matches crew members looking for fantastic positions on ships and boats around the world, from small sailboats and yachts to large commercial ships.

*"Though we travel the world over to find
the beautiful, we must carry it with us, or
we will find it not." ~Ralph Waldo Emerson*

VOLUNTEERING

We are big on volunteering. I (Shelley) volunteer at home, and I've also volunteered around the world – most extensively in India, where I've gone every year for nearly 10 years, volunteering in orphanages. This experience so affected me, that I ended up writing a book about it, and the children I grew to know and love along with the issues that so impacted their lives. Keith has also traveled with me to volunteer at this Indian orphanage – an incredible travel experience for us to share!

Check out Shelley's book (37) about her volunteer travel experiences in India!

Keith spent several weeks in Cambodia in 2012, working with a nonprofit organization to bring digital media and training to very low-income students at a school in Siem Reap. When the two of us were in Cambodia together in 2010, we visited an orphanage and also a temple where the monks ran a sewing school to give women a marketable skill.

So we are both big advocates of volunteering when traveling; it's not only a way to give back and make a difference, but it really connects you with a place, its people and everyday life in a way that few other travel experiences can. This one-of-a-kind cultural immersion is a great way to ensure against "consumerist travel" – that is, only consuming and taking out from a destination you're visiting without really supporting the local communities in a vital way. There is a huge value that is created when people of different cultures learn from and become role models for each other.

If your travel plans include extensive volunteering, check out Jane Stanfield's excellent workbook, *Mapping Your Volunteer Vacation* (38). If you want to find out first-hand what different sorts of volunteer vacations are really like, read *The Voluntary Traveler* (39), a book that Shelley contributed to. This anthology has voluntourism experiences from many different authors, about many different types of volunteering all over the world.

The influx of foreign voluntourists into isolated and/or impoverished communities provides a direct contact with alternative cultural traditions, especially for girls. Think what it could mean to a young girl in a country where child brides are common, to see a woman from another country digging an irrigation ditch and traveling on her own. And more than anything, one of the most surprising aspects of volunteering is usually the end recognition that you have gotten far more out of the experience than you have given.

However, one thing to know is that volunteer travel, or voluntourism as it's sometimes called, does not always mean free travel. In fact, more often than not, it costs just as much as traveling in any other way that would involve purchasing your own airfare, hotel and food. Many people express surprise at this fact, wondering why it is that they have to pay when they are volunteering their time and work to the organization.

Volunteering in India, Nov. 2010

Well, there are very good reasons for this. Non-profit organizations are very grateful, and needful, of your assistance, to be sure. But you need to understand that they are also extremely cash-strapped and always in need of funding, for the most part. Any non-profit that uses volunteers, whether on a local or traveling basis, will tell you that the most expensive part of utilizing volunteers is the initial recruitment and training, which takes a great deal of the organization's time, money and resources. So when you are talking about voluntourism – which typically is done for anywhere from a week to a couple of months – the organization is working with you as a short-term volunteer, and while you are donating your time and work for free, it does cost the organization time and money to organize, orient and train you. In addition, if the non-profit organization also paid the travel expenses for these traveling volunteers, they would likely be in the hole, rather than receiving true volunteer benefits.

So when you start looking at volunteer travel opportunities around the world, know up front that the vast majority of the time you will be paying your own expenses, and it may not be any cheaper than any other form of travel. Of course, as we've stated, the benefits to the organization, the community served, and yourself as the traveler, are well worth it in our opinion. We encourage you strongly to volunteer when you travel.

That said, we will offer some tips for how to best utilize volunteering to travel at a low cost:

- **Incorporate volunteering into existing travel plans.**
Particularly when traveling internationally, the biggest expense with voluntourism is getting there. If you can work volunteering into travel plans you already have, your expenses go way down and your chances of using volunteer work to extend your travels more cheaply, or even for free, go way up.

- **Volunteer for longer, rather than shorter, periods of time.**
The rule of "travel longer, travel cheaper" apply just as much to voluntourism as it does to regular travel. Due to the resource expenditure to the organization discussed above, costs passed along to the volunteer for their expenses are much higher when you are only volunteering for a few days or a couple of weeks. Once you start volunteering for several weeks or months at a time, the organization gets more value for your work in relation to the resources they've spent to set you up, and it's more likely that you will not have very many expenses associated with volunteering. In fact, for longer-term volunteers of a month or more, many organizations will provide you housing and perhaps even some meals at no cost to you.

> Are you a student? Many universities offer volunteer abroad opportunities, many with potential grants or financial assistance. There are also lots of other ways for students to travel for free, including sponsored study abroad and cultural exchanges. Check out The Telegraph UK's story on 10 Ways Students can Globetrot for Free (40).

- **Plan your volunteer route for maximum effectiveness.** When it's time to travel from one place to another, use the internet and low-cost airlines to figure out the best geographical route to take. Start by searching on aggregator sites like Kayak, Wego, Momondo and Skyscanner. Then be sure and check out Which Budget to make sure you are finding the best deals. Often you can just check low-cost tickets or the best deals between countries without putting in specific cities or dates. This will help you figure out the cheapest points to travel, and volunteer, between. For example, going from one place in Europe to another using Ryan Air would almost certainly be inexpensive. Likewise, flying between dozens of Asian cities on Air Asia can be done for EUR 50 or less. By knowing the lowest-cost transportation options ahead of time, you can search for and choose volunteer projects in the destinations that appeal to you.

- **Volunteer with local organizations, and work directly with the organization.** Local, grassroots organizations are where you will find the volunteer opportunities that don't cost you anything, and where benefits such as housing and food might be included. These are pretty easy to find while you're on the road; they often post at hostels and restaurants where backpackers/travelers hang out. Larger, national or global organizations tend to be the ones with higher administrative costs, and therefore higher costs passed on to volunteers. Also, many times it is agencies setting these up on behalf of you and the organization, acting as a sort of matchmaker. Agencies, while mostly legitimate and good agencies, add in fees for their own services and administration costs to your volunteering fee. Working directly with a nonprofit, rather than going through an agency, means you are not spending money on these costs.

- **Check out any organization thoroughly before you commit.** While most non-profits are legitimate and doing good work with transparent accountability, unfortunately there are some bad apples in the bunch. To make sure that your efforts count and you are working with a great organization, you need to exercise due diligence. Ask a lot of questions, and request full disclosure on a breakdown of exactly what all the fees they charge you are going toward. Also find out what percentage of their fees and donated funds go toward administrative costs, and what percentage goes to their clients and direct services. A good charity should have no more than 15% administrative costs, and will have no problem answering all your questions and providing you this information. If they seem reluctant or not forthcoming, that should set off warning bells. You can also check with vetting services such as GlobalGiving.org, that research and investigate non-profits on their own so that volunteers and donors know they are dealing with a legitimate, above-board organization that checks out. Other such organizations include GuideStar.org and CharityNavigator.org (US-based).

- **Follow your passion.** While the previous tips will help you volunteer around the world at a lower cost, don't forget the value that the experience will have for you personally. Don't choose to dig a well in Cambodia just because it's a cheap flight from Thailand, if digging a well isn't something you are going to enjoy. Check out the organisation to ensure that it is legitimate and its mission is something you can really get behind. If you are passionate about human rights, volunteer with refugee services around the globe. If you love children, volunteer at schools and orphanages. If you want to help protect the planet and our animal species, then make sure you choose projects that are doing that work.

With a little thought and planning, you could spend years travelling the world very cheaply, doing good and getting an immense amount of joy and satisfaction in return.

One of the most rewarding experiences I had while traveling was volunteering in Siem Reap, Cambodia. Within 48 hours of arriving, I landed a gig teaching 4 photography classes at an after school program for underprivileged kids at Anjali-House.com. This led to a documentary project photographing the work being done by HaloTrust.org, an organization which removes unexploded land mines.

While traveling in Fiji, I had the good fortune to meet a fellow who was involved in marine conservation. When he found out I was a scuba diver and had an underwater housing, he asked me if I'd like to spend 3 weeks on a private island, including room and board and unlimited diving, in exchange for photos of the work being done by his organization. My response? "When do we leave?"

--John Langford, CozmicCamera.com

Voluntourism Resources:

- Leaving More Than You Take (41) is an article written by Shelley on the subject.
- TheEthicalVolunteer.com is a great site that focuses on both cost effective and ethical volunteering worldwide. They list hostels along with community-drive projects, helping volunteers connect to those projects with no extra costs, on an extremely low budget.
- CharityGuide.org/volunteer/ has a great section on volunteer vacations.
- GVIusa.com features volunteer trips around the world.
- CrossCulturalSolutions.org is a great website for finding international volunteer opportunities.
- GlobalVolunteers.org is perhaps the largest agency for international volunteer opportunities.
- GlobalHelpSwap.com helps people find free volunteering opportunities all over the world.
- BUNAC.org offers a range of volunteer abroad programs worldwide.
- AmericanHiking.org is a good way to incorporate volunteering into travel in the United States, especially for outdoorsy types. There are no costs involved; but accommodations are generally camping, and the work is physical. That said, you get to enjoy beautiful national parks and trails for free, and help maintain them.
- ContinentalDivideTrail.org also lists national park volunteer opportunities that are free, along the Continental Divide Scenic Trail.
- SierraClub.org offers many outdoors conservation opportunities for volunteers, both in the U.S. as well as Central America and other places.
- NationalTrust.org.uk is a similar organization in Great Britian, with 400+ working vacations where you might volunteer on a farm or restoration project, at low rates that include food & housing.

BARTERING

Barter expands buying power. It is successfully used by hotels, airlines, governments, Fortune 500 companies and private enterprises. In today's economy, barter is a $20 billion industry.

We barter frequently for free travel, using our travel writing and photography skills/careers to exchange reviews and publicity for accommodations or tours. But you don't have to be a writer or photographer to have something to barter; many small proprietors will need legal or accounting services, website or brochure design, or even just rooms painted or renovation help.

Individuals can barter, too. You might consider the possibility of bartering a service or skill you have, for travel. This could be your actual profession or business – are you an accountant, lawyer, graphic or website designer, chef, electrician, plumber, printer, consultant...the possibilities for exchanging your professional services for accommodations and other travel perks are limited only by your imagination, and the time it takes to contact desired barter exchangers and offer your proposition. With the right lead time and a little flexibility, booking through a barter exchange is a great way to stretch your dollar. But don't limit yourself to what you do for a living – think about what other skills you have, personally. Photography, writing, brochure design, handyman work, painting, pet sitting, housekeeping and other services are often in demand by businesses. You can also barter goods; people trade everything from cars and boats to cameras, computers, electronic equipment and just about anything of value.

 Barter Resources:

- U-Exchange.com is the largest swap site, with no transaction or membership fees.
- ForBarterTravel.com is a concierge service that keeps a list of travel opportunities that are available for barter. There is a small booking fee for each transaction confirmed.
- IMSbarter.com is a professional barter network for businesses and professionals. Membership is $595, plus commissions.
- BarterNews.com offers many articles and information about bartering, including a section on travel barter.
- Blog.bizx.com is a great blog run by BizXChange, dedicated to the business-to-business barter industry.
- This article on Budget Travel gives a few real life examples of how people bartered for travel (42).

Bartering on your own is usually the most successful with small, independently-owned enterprises. You will more likely broker an exchange for your services with a bed-and-breakfast or family-run inn than a hotel. You can strike barter deals on your own, by simply researching places that you'd like to barter with and calling or emailing them with your offer (be sure to fully describe what you are offering, and preferably include a link to a website that shows your work, if possible, or give samples and references).

There are also websites and services that allow members to create a profile that lists their service or product offerings for barter, and to contact other members. Most of these services charge a membership fee, from nominal to substantial; others are free to sign up and broker a barter agreement, and then take the equivalent of a commission on a successful transaction.

CROWD-FUNDED TRAVEL

Crowdfunding has become very popular in recent years. People use crowdfunding to do all sorts of projects, from recording an album or making a movie to an art installation or starting a nonprofit venture, using websites like Kickstarter. And it's also gained popularity as a way for people to fund their dream trips around the world, specific adventures such as a marathon, or voluntourism projects.

Using websites like IndieGoGo, GoFundMe and Trevolta, travelers set up campaign websites that accept donations and begin raising money for their trip. You might ask, why would your family and friends give you money to go travel? Many people ask for donations instead of birthday presents or wedding registries; or they offer to give something back to the people who donate. Often this is in the form of reporting about the whole experience on a blog or social media, sending photographs or postcards from the trip, or something of value they have to give back in return.

And don't underestimate the power of investing people in your experience. People love to live vicariously, and will often donate to a friend's quest to climb Mount Kilimanjaro, run the Mongolian Rally race or bike across Europe – just to be part of the adventure. This can hold even more true with volunteer projects; people generally have big hearts and will happily donate to a campaign that will send you to help build water wells in Africa or volunteer at a school in

Vietnam. Our friend, Barbara Joubert, is in fact in Madagascar this very moment as this is being written. She had an opportunity to travel with Whole Foods Market's nonprofit, Whole Planet Foundation, on a volunteer trip. Trouble was, she didn't have enough money to cover the trip. She created a GoFundMe campaign (43) and within days had raised over $1,100 and was able to make this amazing journey!

BECOMING A REVIEWER/SHOPPER

There are numerous companies that provide blind shopping services for all kinds of businesses, from hotels to restaurants, retail stores and movie theaters. The professional shopper visits the business just as any other customer would, and reports back on his or her experience. You probably would not be comped or reimbursed for more than one night's stay as a shopper, but it's worth checking into if you're interested in this option. The shopping company typically provides a comprehensive checklist

Photo: Mystery Shopping Providers Assn

and report listing all of the aspects that you need to pay attention to, rate and report on, so there is definitely time and work involved.

To get started with this option, visit MysteryShop.org, where you can learn more and find a list of shopping companies worldwide. Also, CoyleHospitality.com is an organization that specifically provides mystery shopping services to the hospitality industry, including hotels, timeshares, vacation rentals and cruises. A-Closer-Look.com and HotelShoppingNetwork.com are other companies specializing in the hospitality industry, as is. Go to volition.com/mysteryUSA1.html for a full list of various types of shopping services.

CONTESTS AND SWEEPSTAKES

There are a number of travel websites that run contests, drawings and sweepstakes for all kinds of vacations, trips, accommodations, cruises or airline tickets, as well as goods like backpacks and travel gear. Giveaways seem to be even more prevalent with the advent of social media; it seems everyone has a twitter and facebook profile these days, and some of these contests are as simple as sending an email, entering a drawing, filling out a survey, re-tweeting a post or liking a facebook page.

Others involve things such as submitting a paragraph about why you'd like to travel to a certain destination, your favorite vacation, or sending in a great photograph or video from your own travels. Virtually all online travel contests are free to enter; occasionally some will require you to sign up for an email newsletter, trial magazine subscription or similar.

Most of the major airlines and hotel chains frequently run giveaway contests as well, so don't forget to keep your eyes open; signing up for the email newsletters at these websites is a good way to stay apprised of contests. The terrific TravelSweepstakesBlogger.com keeps a list going of travel giveaways worldwide, as do SweepsAdvantage.com, TravelOnion.com, ContestBee.com and ContestGirl.com.

And of course, subscribe to our blog at howtotravelforfree.net – we tell you about the travel contests and sweepstakes we learn about, and run a Friday Travel Dreaming post that recaps the best free travel opportunities every week!

 Some of the major websites that frequently run sweepstakes include:

- WorldNomads.com
- IntrepidTravel.com
- Frommers.com/deals/
- Fodors.com
- Concierge.com/cntraveler/contestsquizzes
- TravelandLeisure.com/travel-blog/
- Islands.com/contests/
- Away.com/free_stuff/index.html
- Win.TravelChannel.com
- NeoTravel.com/free/vacation-contests.php
- Contests.cheapoair.com
- Blog.virtuoso.com/tag/sweepstakes/
- BudgetTravel.com
- NationalGeographic.com
- PeterGreenberg.com/category/travel-contest/

"Travel is never a matter of money, but of courage."
— *Paulo Coehlo*

JOBS, VACATION TIME & SABBATICALS

Of course, when you travel as much as we do and start talking to people about longer-term, far less expensive travel, one of the main topics that come up is that of jobs, and how to get the time off. "That might work for you – you're travel writers/bloggers/photographers!" many people say. Interestingly enough, the assumed impossibility of being able to travel for several weeks, months or even years at a time is the major argument against even contemplating such a thing, nipping possibly some of your best life experiences in the bud before they even become dreams.

http://www.flickr.com/photos/foundphotos

The subject of this book is not how to get the time to travel, or get a new job or career, or save enough money to take off for a year – those topics are books unto themselves, and are covered extensively in other books and websites. The purpose of *this* book is the travel itself – in it, we've shared with you our tactics, resources and tips that we use to travel for free, or very cheaply. Whether you use these tactics to take a one-week vacation, or take a year off and see the world, is up to you.

However, we feel we would be remiss not to at least touch on the subject of work and the time to travel. First of all, let's go back to the rule that we covered at the very beginning of this book:

In general, the longer you can travel for, the less money you spend.

Although it kind of goes against common sense, it's true. Airfare is usually one of the biggest costs when traveling, especially internationally; and so once you get there, that airfare expense gives you a lot more bang for your buck the farther and longer you can travel on it. Also, it's a lot cheaper to rent lodging by the week or month than it is by the night, and when you have more time to spend traveling you can utilize slower – and cheaper – methods such as trains and boats.

Granted, I (Shelley) get to do a lot of travel due to my work as a travel writer; and both our work systems are basically portable, and can be done virtually anywhere there's an internet connection. But you don't have to be a writer for this to be so – in today's world, more and more portability, remote access, virtual offices, consulting and entrepreneurial methods are being used in many jobs, not just the self-employed. You may already be able to combine time off with working remotely from the office, to create more time to travel while you work, than you think possible.

For more information and inspiration on how to fund your travels, incorporate travel with your lifestyle and/or turn your passions into a self-sustaining business, check out these recommended resources:

- 5 Ways to Make Extra Income Online
- Turning a Travel Passion into a Business (44)
- Real Jobs are Overrated (45)
- 5 Secrets to Enjoying the Benefits of Money – Without Having Any (46)
- 10 Round-the-World Travel Myths Debunked (47)
- 25 Great Tips for Planning your Trip, from Top Travel Bloggers (48)

Many people also combine vacation time with negotiated time off without pay, and even paid sabbaticals, to travel. If you've been at your job for a while and are highly valued, you might be surprised at additional time off or a sabbatical that you are able to negotiate. Your employer might even find value in some sort of a learning vacation – would knowing how to speak another language benefit your company? Maybe there's a training program, seminar or retreat in your field somewhere in the world that would give you an edge in your job – and maybe you could tack on a little vacation or personal time for exploring on your own as well.

We have plenty of friends who have regular, full-time, 9-to-5 employment who have traveled extensively around the world, for weeks or months at a time. While they often utilize the tactics just described, another popular method is the work-and-save-money, then don't-work-and-travel plan. Lots of people work for a year or two and save a decent percentage of their salary, to then take off for a few months or a year and travel around. This is exactly what Keith did in 2004, when he traveled around Asia for two years.

You may wonder what such gaps in employment do to your prospects of finding another job when you return – and the answer is, surprisingly little. In fact, when prospective bosses find out the *reason* you've been gone so long, it's often met with admiration, inquisitiveness, and the attitude that it's a benefit on your resume, as if you'd gone back to school for a grad degree. When Keith returned from his hiatus in Asia and began interviewing, he often found that as soon as the subject came up, the interview questions quickly moved from being about the job, to about his travels – people wanted to know everything about it. He had no trouble landing another job quickly.

A career break is a great way to sharpen your hard and soft skills, both of which should be integrated into your discussions with your prospective employer. When it comes to discussing your soft skills, aptitude and attitude, remind your recruiter that you just spent the past few months traveling around the world in which every day you had to figure out where to eat, where to sleep and how to get around, often in countries where you didn't speak the local language. As a result, you are ready to tackle whatever challenges the job has to offer.

--Jeff Jung, CareerBreakSecrets.com

Then, of course, there are the people who love traveling, and want to be in a different kind of place and doing a different kind of thing so much, that they follow their passions to create a new career. Think accountants turned scuba instructors, or the corporate refugee who now leads treks in Nepal.

WHEN WAS THE *last* TIME YOU DID SOMETHING FOR THE *first* TIME?

bootsnall.com/rtw

The point is, whether you are able to work remotely, save money and then take off for longer trips, run your own business or start a new career – the only limits are your imagination. Get creative and brainstorm the possibilities! And even if you absolutely love the job you have and would never give it up for the world, this book should have given you a lot of resources for stretching your travel farther on far, far fewer dollars – even if that is for two weeks a year.

Bon voyage!

"The whole object of travel is not to set foot on foreign land; it is at last to set foot on one's own country as a foreign land.
~*G. K. Chesterton*

We sincerely hope you have enjoyed this book, and that the ideas and tips in it, and our own travel practices and experiences, will help you travel more and better, for a lot less money.

Please feel free to contact us if you have any questions or suggestions about this book – or if you would like to access more travel resources and articles:

www.shelleyseale.com
Shelley Seale, Travel Journalist & Author

http://travelsherpakeith.com
Keith Hajovsky, Travel Consultant & Photographer

WEBSITE REFERENCE LIST

Below is a list of all the long URL webpages that we have referenced throughout the book:

1. Tim Leffel's Cheapest Destinations Blog:
    http://www.cheapestdestinationsblog.com/
2. Complain the right way:
    http://travelforfreebook.wordpress.com/2013/05/13/flight-problem-complain-the-right-way-to-rake-in-mileage-points/
3. Keith's interview at The Washington Times:
    http://communities.washingtontimes.com/neighborhood/donnes-world/2010/dec/27/tips-new-year-how-travel-budget-travel-sherpa-keit/
4. Boarding Area article:
    http://boardingarea.com/viewfromthewing/2012/01/07/how-to-use-hidden-city-and-throwaway-ticketing-to-save-money-on-airfare/
5. Wikipedia's list of low-cost airlines:
    http://en.wikipedia.org/wiki/List_of_low-cost_airlines
6. Lonely Planet's Thorn Tree forum:
    http://www.lonelyplanet.com/thorntree/index.jspa
7. Are budget airlines really cheaper?: http://flashpackerfamily.com/are-budget-airlines-really-cheaper/
8. Greg and Angie Rose RV story:
    http://travelforfreebook.wordpress.com/2012/01/13/the-roses-travel-throughout-north-america-on-the-cheap/
9. International Ferry Directory: http://routesinternational.com/ships.htm
10. Washington Times Ferry Story:
    http://www.washingtontimes.com/news/2008/jul/03/ferry-travel-prone-to-accidents/
11. Budget travel by bike: http://www.bootsnall.com/articles/12-02/cycling-the-world-on-14-per-day.html
12. Paris Biking Story:
    http://www.businessweek.com/globalbiz/content/nov2007/gb2007112_574198.htm
13. Treehugger Article: http://www.treehugger.com/files/2008/09/bike-sharing-goes-global-5-bike-sharing-programs-to-know-about.php
14. Shelley's interview at The Washington Times:
    http://communities.washingtontimes.com/neighborhood/donnes-world/2010/nov/1/home-exchanges-deliver-travel-savings-and-authenti/
15. Transitions Abroad Home Exchange Article:
    http://www.transitionsabroad.com/listings/travel/home_exchanges/articles/home-exchanges-enrich-travel-experience.shtml
16. Huffington Post housesitting story:
    http://www.huffingtonpost.com/dalene-heck/how-to-travel-the-world-for-free_b_3590595.html
17. Budget Travel's couchsurfing article:
    http://www.budgettravel.com/blog/confessions-of-a-couchsurfer,12936/
18. Canvas Holidays FamilyExtra; http://www.canvasholidays.co.uk/camping-holidays/family-holidays/familyextra
19. Canvas Holidays free guide to camping:
    http://www.canvasholidays.co.uk/why-canvas-holidays/guide-to-camping

20. Travelling Two wild camping tips: http://travellingtwo.com/resources/wild-camping-a-few-tips
21. BootsnAll best places to camp: http://www.bootsnall.com/articles/12-08/best-places-to-camp-around-the-world.html
22. Women staying in monasteries: http://www.women-on-the-road.com/stay-in-a-monastery.html
23. Monastery Inns in the US: http://bandb.about.com/cs/uniquegetaways/a/monastery.htm
24. 15 great monastery stays around the world: http://matadornetwork.com/trips/15-monastery-stays-worldwide/
25. USA Today monastery article: http://traveltips.usatoday.com/stay-monastery-europe-103363.html
26. Airbnb cool places to stay: https://www.airbnb.com/wishlists/unique-places-to-stay
27. EHow Hotel Points Article: http://www.ehow.com/how_5512822_turn-airline-miles-hotel-stays.html
28. The best jobs to pay for your travel: http://travelforfreebook.wordpress.com/2013/04/10/the-best-jobs-that-can-pay-for-your-travel/
29. BootsnAll funding travel message boards: boards.bootsnall.com/funding-your-travel-habit-f54.html
30. Wand'rly making a living on the road: http://wandrlymagazine.com/article/the-oregon-coast/make-a-living-on-the-road/
31. How to make money while traveling: http://trekhound.com/2012/04/16/how-to-make-money-while-traveling/
32. USA Today on traveling free on a sailboat: http://traveltips.usatoday.com/travel-sailboat-103386.html
33. CNN on sailing the world for free: http://www.cnn.com/2013/08/26/travel/how-to-sail-around-world/index.html?hpt=hp_c3
34. Nora Dunn's financial travel tips: http://www.theprofessionalhobo.com/category/financial-travel-tips/
35. Interview with Chris Guillebeau: http://travelforfreebook.wordpress.com/2012/10/09/the-100-startup-travel-more-and-live-the-life-you-want/
36. Matador's article about work camping: http://matadornetwork.com/abroad/travel-for-free-as-a-work-camper/
37. Shelley's book, The Weight of Silence: http://weightofsilence.wordpress.com
38. Mapping Your Volunteer Vacation: http://www.janestanfieldwish.com
39. The Voluntary Traveler: http://astore.amazon.com/theweiofsil-20/detail/0980232368
40. 10 ways students can globetrot for free: http://www.telegraph.co.uk/education/universityeducation/student-life/9764605/University-travel-10-ways-students-can-globe-trot-for-free.html
41. Leaving More Than You Take Article: http://content.yudu.com/Library/A1ju6n/OMTimesMagazineJanua/resources/112.htm
42. Bartering for travel: http://www.budgettravel.com/feature/0905_HTTN_Barter,6066/

43. Barbara Joubert's GoFundMe campaign:
http://www.gofundme.com/barbarainmadagascar
44. 5 ways to make extra income online:
http://b2b.meetplango.com/2012/07/travel-passion-business/
45. Real jobs are overrated: http://www.bootsnall.com/articles/13-04/real-jobs-are-overrated.html
46. 5 secrets to enjoying money without having any:
http://www.vagabondish.com/secrets-enjoying-benefits-money/
47. 10 round the world travel myths debunked:
http://www.bootsnall.com/articles/11-07/10-round-the-world-travel-myths-debunked.html
48. 25 great tips from travel bloggers:
http://www.thebarefootnomad.com/travel-tips/25-great-tips-for-planning-your-trip-from-top-travel-bloggers/

33977998R00061

Made in the USA
Lexington, KY
17 July 2014